DANCING IN THE STREET

The Homecoming, 1942.

We paused by the harmonium in the hall.

David and I longed to pull out all the stops.

'Not tonight children,' Molly sighed.

The last time we slept in our house was between our parents on a mattress on the kitchen floor; Jim had arrived home unexpectedly that night. We listened to the thunder of the ack-ack guns and drone of enemy planes overhead. Tonight we would be in our own beds.

Molly turned the light low. She kissed us goodnight. 'Nice to be home, isn't it...' *I was a Big Girl now.*

DANCING IN THE STREET

by

Sheila Newberry

Dales Large Print Books
Long Preston, North Yorkshire,
BD23 4ND, England.

British Library Cataloguing in Publication Data.

Newberry, Sheila
    Dancing in the street.

    A catalogue record of this book is
    available from the British Library

    ISBN   978-1-84262-859-1 pbk

Published in Large Print 2011 by arrangement with
Sheila Newberry, care of Judith Murdoch Literary Agency

Dales Large Print is an imprint of Library Magna Books Ltd.

Printed and bound in Great Britain by
T.J. (International) Ltd., Cornwall, PL28 8RW

Dedicated: to two unforgettable teachers, who signed my essays, AEC and FF.

Also for 'Maggie'

Foreword

Readers of my previous memoirs by Dales, *Knee Deep in Plums*, *Come You On Inside*, *Seven Pounds of Potatoes Please* and *Who Stirs the Porridge in the Pot?* may have wondered about the gap years after my early childhood, through grammar school, to working in London in the 1950's.

Most of my school friends were film fans, well, I had my idol, too, Disraeli – FF was responsible for that – she was a charismatic history teacher, who wrote her capital F's like continental sevens... AEC, affectionately known as 'Auntie', who taught us English language and literature, understood the dreamers – I imagine she too was one, when she was a child.

Those who would like to know more about life in the suburbs under the shadow of the great Crystal Palace, during the Nineteen Thirties to Fifties, might care to read my story *The Family at Number Five*. (Piatkus, hard back; Harlequin Mills & Boon, paper back; and Magna large print editions, all available from Amazon, or the library.) Glory, the little girl in the book, has many of the same experiences as me, including being captivated by the image of Disraeli.

Sheila Newberry.

ONE

The Homecoming

Molly, our mum, David and I returned to Surrey in 1942. We had been bombed out in November, 1940, after witnessing the Battle of Britain in the skies overhead. The past two years had been spent in Suffolk with my aunt Dolly and her family, while our father remained in Bath with the Admiralty personnel who had been evacuated there at the beginning of the war.

We travelled by train, having to stand most of the way in the corridor, to Liverpool Street Station, which was crowded with men in uniform, laden with heavy kitbags. We queued for what seemed hours for a bus home, were driven through ravaged London streets and were relieved when the windows misted up with fine rain, obscuring our view. As usual I began to feel sick, and my head drooped on to Molly's shoulder to rest against her fox fur tippet, which smelled of mothballs. The black beady eyes of the fox (what a horrible fashion this was) were frightening, though I was no longer a baby, but at that moment I was too nauseous to care.

Our house had been patched up, with temporary ceilings, new windows and doors, there was an odour of neglect, of damp: silver fish scuttled across the floors, books left piled on the shelves, old friends which I immediately turned to, had rust marks on pages and corners nibbled by mites, or maybe mice. To me, this didn't feel like home any more. Although it was early September, we all felt chilled. There was a recent fall of soot in the hearth, a reminder of the aftermath of the bomb, when our little white dog was black with coal dust.

The first thing Molly did was to put on

one bar of the electric fire in the living room. We weren't due a delivery of coal yet. Shivering, but not complaining, we made toast, scorching slices of bread left over from the journey, and drank tepid tea from the flask. We had brought a few provisions with us, but although the electricity had been restored, as yet there was no gas: Molly couldn't use the New World cooker as she'd intended. She'd looked forward to this, after managing with a gas ring in the hearth in the cottage; nor could she light the geyser for a bath.

There were beds to make up, cases to unpack. That was our homecoming.

The grandfather clock under the stair well, damaged by the blast, no longer chimed, but it was still there. We glanced in the front room before climbing the stairs to bed. The carpet was rolled up under the window, the settee and chairs shrouded in dust sheets. The piano, which Jim's parents had given him and Molly as a wedding gift, had survived. All these familiar things had been in storage until Jim paid a brief visit to the house the previous week to see them reinstalled. He'd endured hours of driving, some of it in the blackout, after calling in on us at Dolly's to pick up the heavy trunk and a couple of cases of clothes. I knew something was up, but we were sent to school as usual, and only saw our dad briefly. I think Molly was afraid I would make a fuss, for Dolly was like a second mother to me, little Jassy like a sister, and I loved country life, although, of course, I missed my father.

Now, we paused by the harmonium in the hall. David and I looked at each other, each wanting to be first to pull out all the stops.

'Not tonight children,' Molly sighed.

The last time we slept in our house, I remembered, we lay between our parents, on a mattress on the kitchen floor, for Jim had arrived home unexpectedly that night, listening to the thunder of the ack-ack guns and the drone of enemy planes overhead. Tonight, we would be in our own beds.

The new bedroom suite Molly had been

so proud of, had been smashed to pieces when my parents' bedroom received the full impact of the bomb. Jim had acquired a double bed for their room from somewhere, but otherwise it was empty of furniture. David and I had our single beds in the back bedroom, his with the Cambridge blue bedspread, mine draped in Oxford blue, as we were rivals in the Boat Race. The Edwardian wardrobe and dressing table had been painted pink by Molly to 'freshen them up' just before the war. The wardrobe had an open compartment for 'hats', ideal for me to keep my own books. I would unpack them from their box first thing tomorrow, I promised myself.

Molly turned the little nightlight low. She bent over each bed to kiss us goodnight. 'Nice to be home, isn't it...'

I murmured, 'Yes, Mummy,' because I knew that was what she wanted to hear.

Many of the neighbouring houses remained boarded up: the Motts next door were still away. We'd come home because my brother had a place at a grammar school in Croydon in September, and I was due to sit the scholarship next Spring.

The schools had finally reopened, three years after they were closed, following one or two false starts. Things were quiet on the Home Front. Our local school had small classes, few teachers, as the majority of children evacuated at the outbreak of war had not returned. Some had lost their homes: the rubble had been cleared, but gaps between the houses had created little overgrown alleyways for us curious children to explore. Before the war, we'd not been allowed to play in the street, nor during our first homecoming, just before the Blitz, as Molly deemed it too hazardous. In Suffolk we had roamed freely.

Now, the only danger of being 'run over' as Molly put it, was from the occasional bicycle or highly unlikely, by a runaway milkman's horse, if the horse was startled when rooting in his nose-bag outside a customer's house.

Cars were a rare sight these days due to the shortage of petrol and the fact that most drivers between eighteen and forty, except for those in reserved occupations, were serving in the forces. The only women about were mothers of young children and the elderly. Those with children over ten years old were drafted into war work...

At first I didn't venture far from home – just across the road to where there was a large blank wall, known as *Henry's*, where I practised playing with a couple of old tennis balls, a game called *Sevenses*, which required bouncing the balls and chanting in a sing-song way: *Goering is Boring! Goebbels throws snowballs!* were two of the 'calypsos' of the day. I was not alone, but it wasn't a team game. The girls who joined me were new-comers, Londoners, as empty houses were requisitioned for the homeless at this time. The relentless thump of the ball against the wall drove the bald man who worked in the courtyard beyond (at what, we never dis-covered) to appear from round the side of the house to shout furiously, 'Clear off!' We never answered him back, but ran away, with the balls stuffed up our knickers. We would return in a day or two. Our mothers didn't discourage us, as they could see us from the upstairs windows.

I still missed the countryside, the walks across the meadows, the glimpses of wild life – but I was adapting slowly. There were few dogs around now, for many of these had been taken to the vets and put to sleep at the beginning of the war, when the evacuation had commenced, and again, when the bombing led to many stray ownerless animals. Cats were everywhere, often thin and abandoned, and I adopted a black tom whom I named Timoshenko after a prominent Russian of the time. We still had our Pekinese, Waggles, though the only walks he enjoyed were in my doll's pram, and I was getting too old for that. David had his white mice in the garage: he sold the offspring at 6d. each, but after hiding them in his desk at school, had been told to cease trading.

16

Despite the mice doing tricks, like balancing on a string between chairs, I didn't care to hold them as I didn't like their long, pink tails, and their incontinence. Timoshenko blinked his golden eyes, and purred on my lap, while waiting his chance. Plain old house-mice were opportunists, too. David soon had 'rare' brown and white mice which were much prized by the local boys. His money box was soon far heavier than mine.

Our semi-detached end-of-row house, with attached garage, was part of a small suburban estate built between the wars, off a pleasant green lane of rather grand Edwardian houses and Victorian villas, where it was rumoured there were still parlour maids and gardeners. Our street, like the others on the so called white collar estate, was named after a famous general of the Boer War. It was convenient for all the amenities. It was a ten minute walk to the clock tower, the high street with that wonderful store, Woolworths, and the Pavilion, known to all as the 'Pav', our local cinema. This was next to the Municipal Swimming baths. Turn right at the Clock and you came to the main-line station to London. Further down was the Library, which due to my new-found freedom, I was able to visit most days. I usually began reading the first of my two books on the way home, often bumping into a lamp-post or someone hurrying to catch a tram, when I would be sternly reminded: 'Look where you're going!' I recall reading poems aloud as I walked along, *'Fair Imogen'* was a favourite: why hadn't my parents called me that? I loved the name.

I met an elderly lady further up our road who invited me in for biscuits and a glass of milk. 'Do you like Westerns?' she asked. I hadn't read one, but I'd seen Hopalong Cassidy at the Pav, also the Lone Ranger and heard his call: 'Heigh ho, Silver!' to his horse. I was thus introduced to the novels of Zane Grey, who roamed the Wild Frontier. Miss W lent me all the books in turn.

Molly preferred the travelling library,

which called once a week. For tuppence a book, she chose half-a dozen novels by her favourite authors like Pearl S Buck. The bookman staggered up the path, carrying these, and then spread his selection halfway up our stairs, chatting to Molly while she inspected the books. He was a little man with a 'pencil' moustache, with a mouthful of brown stained teeth, due to puffing an evil smelling pipe. He looked at me as if he wished I would vanish, and reminded me: 'I do not have books for children.' I would sneakily read these love stories when I got a chance, retrieving them from under the cushion in Molly's chair when I had exhausted my own library books. They had titles like *'A Woman's Way,' 'Stormy Petrel'*, and *'Thursday's Child.'* I knelt by the chair, with my face close to the printed pages and read every word. I was in a world of my own, so Molly said.

TWO

Bread Buns And Big Girls

We had our own parade of local shops on the way to the school, where I was about to join The Big Girls, divided from The Big Boys by a high fence. The children spied on each other through the knotholes.

At the end of our row of houses was the police station, surrounded by a low brick wall. It was a ritual for me to walk along the top of this wall, before jumping down to cross the road to the baker's shop on the corner.

Before the war I could just remember the lovely cakes always on show in the window: now, there was a tray of bread buns which cost a penny each, you could count the currants, and once I found only three – and the National loaf, greyish rather than white. Molly had brought us up on brown bread before the war, but I thought longingly of soft white bread and real butter, of the special treat of a thick crust cut from the crusty loaves still been available in the village bakers.

Skirting the off-licence, where on special Sundays we bought a bottle of Tizer, we came to the corner Tobacconists, run by two sisters who lived with their brother, who worked in London, but sometimes served customers on a Saturday morning. All three were middle-aged and kindly. Kit was the younger sister, who Molly and her friend May agreed, 'has become rather skittish, since the war. Did you see the bow in her hair?' Kit kept packets of Players under the counter for any servicemen who might be on leave. Molly and May exchanged local gossip with Kit while she passed over their 'Five Craven A, please.'

We bought our sweets from a shop called Bob's. Mrs Bob (I don't think that was her name) helped us juggle our sweet coupons. After biting off the stem of my liquorice pipe, I looked at the selection of second-hand magazines and comics spread on the counter. These were sold for a penny each, and if you returned them in good order, you were given a halfpenny in return. The comics were sold again at the original price. I wonder how many times they changed hands? Mrs Bob saved me copies of *The Girls Crystal*, which cost tuppence, having more reading matter.

I loved those magazines and the serials, and unlike the comics, didn't part with them. As toys were in short supply, Mrs Bob took a small commission from selling hand-knitted soft toys – kangaroos in striped wool were a favourite, because in the pouch was a tiny knitted Joey. There was also the occasional wooden train or bricks in a box on wheels, made by a granddad. Mrs Bob kept things under the counter too, like lemonade powder, which she measured by the spoonful into poke bags she fashioned herself from pieces of newspaper. We dipped a forefinger in the acid crystals and licked blissfully – gaining a bright yellow tongue in the process. Ice cream wafers, soft and tasting rather unpleasant, for ice creams had long ago disappeared, were fourteen a penny. We were always hungry, so they filled us up. Cough sweets were not rationed, but tasted horrible when the sugar coating was sucked off.

Half way up the parade was the shop where you could buy newspapers and stationery. This shop was busiest on a Sunday, when the other shops were closed, as the proprietors were Jewish. We bought coloured pencils, pencil sharpeners and boxes of paint from Mrs. Morris. When I was older, I bought deckled-edged writing paper with envelopes lined with blue tissue, and a bottle of purple ink. I had many pen friends. I also spent my pocket money once on a pencil sharpener, which had a blade like a guillotine, which was confiscated almost immediately by Jim next time he was home, as a dangerous object.

Set back was the greengrocers – where there were lengthy queues for vegetables on Saturday mornings, I stood with Molly, listening to the artless chat of young factory workers with their hair still in steel curlers under turbans, which they combed into a frizz later, for Saturday night dances in the church hall. I was reminded of the Land girls billeted with my grandparents, who sounded the same. They went to the dances in pairs, men were in short supply, so the taller of the two girls would 'lead' the shorter in a waltz or quickstep. It was either Victor Sylvester on the wind-up gramophone, or a cheerful matron thumping on the piano.

The fruit-and-veg sisters were Amazons, over six foot tall, and cheerful, decanting potatoes with small clods of earth into our baskets with a smile. They lifted great boxes with ease. They had taken over from their brothers when they joined up. I couldn't remember what bananas tasted like, there were none available nowadays, but an orange was an occasional treat, cut in two between my brother and me. We had fun making 'false teeth' from the pith. When we had colds, Molly would poke a hole in an orange, and insert a precious sugar cube. 'Suck the juice,' she told us, 'and you'll soon feel better.' Eggs were another rare treat, we missed the ones we'd collected warm from the nest, with a stray feather clinging, in the country. Dried egg, mostly scrambled, was not the same at all.

On the other side of the road, the shops were less interesting, though Molly lingered in all of them at times, while I fidgeted and wished we were in Mrs Bob's shop. There was the chemist, who mixed potions and lotions and dispensed free advice on our ailments. Boxes of Dr William's pink pills, intrigued me. Did they taste like cachous? There was liquorice there too, but it was hard and bitter and used as a laxative. Chilblain ointment was sold in little round cardboard boxes. It didn't work though, as we discovered when we anointed our itching toes.

The grocery shop was like a long, dimly lit cavern, with dusty sacks, boxes of biscuits, mouse traps, a wire cheese cutter and scissors to cut the coupons from our ration books. Some things, like tinned fruit were on 'points', and sugar was measured into stiff blue bags with the tops turned over. The grocer, Mr Noble, so an older resident told us, had started out with a stall on the pavement, between the wars. He was cheap and cheerful then, and he still did his best for the regular customers despite all the shortages. Molly called in there most days after she met me from school for one or two items, like Force Flakes, Fairy Soap, and Typhoo Tea. I pointed out the jars of salmon and shrimp paste, my favourite spread at teatime.

We usually just looked in the window of the drapers' shop, but one afternoon we stepped inside to the pealing of a bell. I was hopeful Molly would buy something today so I could watch the little cash container whizzing along the wire overhead to the cashier's desk. Back it would come with the change, often a farthing for most prices ended in 'eleven-three' the pence and farthings after the shillings.

Molly had received a letter from Dolly that morning and we were delighted when she told David and me at breakfast that her sister was coming the following day to stay – 'just for a day or two.'

'Oh, goody, is Jassy coming?'

'Not this time, Auntie Rum next door is looking after her.'

Now, Molly took the letter from the bag and read out from a list.

Miss Winterbourne opened drawers below the counter and placed some small items on the counter. A pink knitted matinee coat, matching leggings, bonnet, bootees and mittens. Baby clothes. Molly counted the money in her purse. 'Have you a little cotton nighty?' Dolly had sent some coupons, it seemed.

'One's not much use,' said Miss Winterbourne, who though she was unmarried was
conversant with infant needs. 'I've a pre-war
one that's shop-soiled. I'll throw that in,
shall I?'

I was curious. Who on earth were these
things for? Was Dolly having a baby? A
thought struck me: Wouldn't it be wonderful if I was going to have a little sister at last!
But then I realised, you don't know what a
baby will be, boy or girl, until it's born, and
Mummy hasn't said anything to us...

All Molly said, as we walked home with
our parcel, neatly tied with string, was,
'While Dolly's here, we're going to see a
friend in London, who has just had a baby.
Don't worry, we'll be back before you arrive
home in the afternoon from school.'

I was adapting to the routine in The Big
Girls, as David was his new school. He had
to leave earlier than me in the mornings to
catch a bus from the Clock, and in the
evenings he had homework awaiting his
attention in his satchel. At night, he often

woke me up when he came to bed, for he stayed up later than me, as he recited his Latin verbs. 'Hic, Hoc, Hec' – I pulled the covers over my ears.

My new teacher, Miss Lancaster, was very stern. She had a profile like the Red Indians described in the Zane Grey Westerns: a hooked nose and jet black hair swept back into a tight knot in the nape of her neck. I felt apprehensive whenever she fixed her gaze on me, in the front row. The first day I joined her class, she swooped down on me, long forefinger jabbing at my copy work.

'You! Why are you printing? You should be doing joined-up writing by now!'

'We – only did printing, at my last school...' I faltered.

'Ridiculous!' With a pencil she drew curves between all my letters. 'Follow that, and don't let me see that infantile printing again!'

My neighbour whispered: 'Loops on your g's and y's - look at mine.' But it wasn't as easy as that, as I soon discovered.

I was in the top class, and Miss L was determined that every child should leave the Big Girls able to read and write. Some had problems due to evacuation, a few were naturally slow. Miss L picked out a team to coach the less able: as I tried to remain inconspicuous after being exposed as one who couldn't do joined-up writing, I was surprised to become one of the pupil teachers. The girl who sat next to me, Anne, was also appointed. I helped two girls, and Anne took charge of two boys. Both Anne and I found it a very rewarding experience and talk about it still.

I made another lifelong friend in the Big Girls' class, a vivacious small girl called Maggie, with beautiful dark red hair flowing down her back. She has to this day an infectious husky giggle and suffered from chronic asthma, but she was full of fun, we had a lot in common, both loving books, writing and painting.

However, around this time, I found difficulty in reading what was written on the blackboard, despite being so close to it. Goodness knows why I didn't tell anyone, but others who developed short sight around the same age have told me they kept this worry to themselves, too. I recall whispering to Anne, 'Can you tell me what Miss Lancaster has written for us to copy?' and Anne looking at me as if I'd lost my marbles. 'What is this world if full of care, We have no time to stop and stare,' she hissed.

'No talking!' barked Miss Lancaster.

Yet at this time, as much later I discovered, the fierce Miss L kept every one of my compositions to encourage the next generation or two of Big Girls in creative writing. When I learned that, I wished I had been privileged to know her better...

Back to Dolly's visit: and again, I heard about this years later – she and Molly visited their young friend Lily in a Salvation Army Home for Mothers and Babies. Lily had become pregnant while working in London, the soldier responsible turned out to be married, and Lily had just given birth to a baby daughter. The kindly people who cared for her and helped her through it all, thought that adoption was the best option. Lily agreed, but when she saw her baby she knew she could never part with her. 'I could leave here,' she cried, 'but I haven't anywhere to go...'

Molly followed her mother's example, who took an old friend home after visiting her in the workhouse. She wrote to Jim, and by return post was told, 'Yes, old dear, let them come to you. Lily will be company for you, while I am away...'

A week later, I came in from school to find Molly and Lily together, with baby Jenny in a rush basket. Jenny was, of course, dressed all in pink!

THREE

Disraeli And Me

September 1943.

I was no longer a Big Girl. I felt very small indeed on my first day at my new school.

There were Big Girls everywhere, and quite a few in my class, it seemed. Big Girls in gymslips and school ties, whereas Molly had decided it was still warm enough for me to wear a summer dress. Before the war, the girls had worn dresses in fine cream-coloured tussore, material which was no longer available. Molly did her best with more substantial cotton, in beige. Such a light shade was totally impractical for school wear. The dresses were too short when she finished sewing, so she lengthened them with false hems. I inherited David's navy gabardine mackintosh, which could be buttoned on either side, but I was conscious it had been worn by a boy before me. We could choose between a pudding basin hat or a beret: I opted for the latter which lasted my entire school days. I intended to jump on it, when I left school, but Jim appropriated it to protect his bald head when painting the house.

A class photograph of the new intake of girls was taken by a teacher. I am among 'the shrimps' at the front, recognisable by my untidy mop of blonde hair. A note was sent to my mother: 'Girls should have short hair, or restrain long hair.' Thereafter, I wore bunches, tied firmly with ribbon, and for years after I left school my hair parted down the middle at the back, where Molly's comb had made a groove. At least I escaped having cropped hair, unlike my friend Maggie, now divested of her crowning glory. I cried with her, for her loss. I was glad though to have Maggie with me as, although she was even smaller than me (she still is petite), she

34

gave me a nudge when I indulged in too much daydreaming. The other girl from our old school was Anne, who soon established herself as top of the class. Anne was also sporty which helped her popularity, and she looked out for me when larger girls teased me about always missing the ball in games. This was because I couldn't see it until it passed my nose.

I chose which school I wanted to go to when the 11+ results came through – it was always called the scholarship then. As an insurance against not passing (my half-joined up writing was a drawback) I also sat the entrance exam to a fee-paying girls' school. I overheard my parents, when Jim had a rare weekend at home, discussing what economies would have to be made if I were to go there, and this worried me. It was a well-established school; David was thriving in the companion boys' school, which had a very good reputation for academic success. I said firmly that I didn't want to go there, but not the reason why. I rejected the offer of a bicycle as a reward for success (I already knew I would never make a cyclist) and asked instead for a puppy! Poor old Waggles had an untimely end when someone threw chicken bones into our garden and he gobbled them up. Jim's landlady's dog had just had a litter of pups, and so I was given my first little Jack Russell. I called her Dinkie. I wasn't aware then, that my parents received several letters from the exclusive school, asking them to change their mind. Apparently, the Head had been impressed by an essay I wrote (entirely from my imagination) about the thrills of an aeroplane trip from Croydon Airport! However, I never regretted the choice I made.

Pupils who had been evacuated with my new school at the beginning of the war, were gradually trickling back. Others who joined Class 1 were a year or two older having come home to take the scholarship later, at thirteen instead of eleven. Teachers too, appeared during my first term, including 'Auntie' who had been further delayed by breaking her collar bone. I think Maggie and I were disappointed at first, because we had enjoyed a stand-in form mistress, a jolly gym teacher who we all admired, in her green Grecian tunic. She taught us country dancing, too, and like the amusing Joyce Grenfell song, when she partnered you, it was embarrassingly 'bust to bust' – or should I say chest, for all the skinny Lizzies? The curvaceous teacher departed to a boys' school with some alacrity. I imagine she was even more popular there.

AEC, that middle-aged lady with curly, dark hair, and two pairs of glasses which she invariably mixed up, ribbed lisle stockings, sensible laced up shoes and tweedy costumes, soon won us over. She was the kindest teacher I have known; she was rarely cross, and her English lessons were inspiring. She really was like everyone's favourite 'aunt.'

Our school was modern, and well-equipped, although not in a very salubrious area. We had to run the gamut of youngsters from the housing estate who bombarded us with snowballs in winter, trying to dislodge our hats, as we walked down the road to the school. Woe betide any girl seen by a teacher not wearing her hat. That was punishable with a discredit mark against your name.

There was a grand Assembly Hall with a curtained stage and piano, where the music teacher, who closed her eyes when she touched the keys, swayed back and forth on her stool, as she played the hymns. Faces were red when the school song was announced on special occasions: *St Patrick's Breastplate* – any sniggers were quelled by the stern Head.

Until I had my first pair of glasses, I was frequently lost within the school – it seemed so vast. There were quadrangles outside the class windows, long corridors and stairs leading upwards on one side to the Science Lab. and on the other to the Art Room. There was a wing which housed the Domestic Science room; off that was the library. Stairs led to a flat where girls learned how to make beds, clean the bath and shine silver, with pink gritty paste on a saucer. The flat was used by teachers on fire-watch duty at various times during the war. Beyond this complex was the dining hall and the kitchens where I became reluctantly acquainted with school dinners...

There were junior and senior cloakrooms, a staff room, from which billowed smoke from many cigarettes, each time the door opened; the Head's study, and a well-equipped gymnasium. Later, showers were installed – purgatory to me and others. We never had enough time to dress before the bell shrilled. The lost property box (items were sold end of term) brimmed with towels, knickers and socks.

Outside was the field, partly given over to Dig for Victory, and a shelter which had been erected at the beginning of the war in the games area, where only the netball posts remained.

The jolly gym teacher was replaced by a much sterner individual. She took a dislike to me almost immediately. I'd enjoyed country dancing sessions, despite being almost smothered by the jolly one's bust at times. The only thing the two teachers had in common was the Grecian tunic which hung loosely on Miss GT's lean figure. She came silently into the hall on that first day carrying a bunch of wooden swords. I was blamed when my insecurely thrust baton at the end of the sword dance caused the shield which was held aloft to fall apart and my fellow dancers to scatter.

'Your name?' Miss GT commanded. I murmured a reply. 'I shall remember that,' she intoned ominously. And she did, to the day I left the school...

I resumed dancing classes on Saturday mornings in the Applegarth Hall, near my home, with a glamorous lady called Joan – known professionally as Cherry. Joan had been involved in an horrific car accident at the beginning of the war, and was unable to return to the stage. She always had hopes of discovering a young prodigy; however, although most of her pupils loved tap dancing and the routines, very few rose on their points. Joan's mother played the piano with great gusto. Molly no doubt breathed a sigh of relief that I wasn't stuck at home with my nose in a book, but I still feared every lesson, in or out of the school gym, with caustic comments on my ineptitude from Miss GT.

I wasn't the only one with defective eyesight. Class 1 had a Medical in the Sick Room in the middle of our first term. Our mothers were summoned to attend. We were used now to the indignity of parading in our fleece lined brown knickers and vests, for this was our sports garb, in the gym and in the field. It was a cold day, I recall, and there was much exaggerated shivering. My fingers were numb and white as they always were in chilly weather. When my name was called, I was measured in height and girth, weighed, and the size of my feet was noted. Girls with large feet got extra clothing coupons, unfortunately, mine were too small.

Then came the dreaded eye test. I gazed intently at what appeared to be a blank chart on the wall. 'Read down as far as you can,' I was instructed. I screwed up the uncovered eye. 'H' I guessed. 'T', the nurse prompted. The other eye was uncovered. Well, I did get the 'T' right, this time.

The doctor was furious with my poor mother. 'Didn't you observe this child is half-blind?' It was a tactless thing to say.

Poor Molly had tears in her eyes. 'She's always reading – she never said...' She turned to me: 'Why ever didn't you tell me you couldn't see properly?'

I had no answer for that. I felt I was being admonished for something I couldn't help.

Shortly afterwards, there were half a dozen girls wearing glasses, including both my friends, though they only needed them for reading. Molly made sure I had attractive frames, for which I was grateful. Two other memories are stirred by recalling that humiliating eye test: I had drops in my eyes at the clinic, which took ages to wear off. I went to the sweet shop – and cannoned into the iron struts of the blind, being cleaned by the owner, and nearly knocked myself out... However, the other memory makes me smile. 'The first thing I did after I got *my* glasses,' Molly said, 'Was to go to the Pictures. I couldn't believe how clearly I could see the screen... I'll take you this Saturday afternoon to the Pav.'

This was an unexpected treat. I didn't have to peer from the front row in the cinema, but sat a few rows back. The film was A.J. Cronin's *Hatter's Castle*, with James Mason menacing in the lead role. There was a seduction scene, and poor Molly kept whispering in my ear, 'Can you see all right?' and me answering, 'Yes Mummy, *perfectly!*'

The subjects I liked best at school were English Language and Literature with dear Auntie; Art, with Helen who wore fishnet stockings and blue eyeshadow, another un-conventional young woman, who was a friend of FF, she who made History come alive; French, with Mademoiselle, who suffered from catarrh and taught us to roll our 'r's', while looking in a hand mirror – 'gargle, girls, gargle!' she encouraged; Geography – except I never could tell Africa from India, you must admit they are both pear-shaped! I once had top marks for writing about the Eskimos, illustrated with an igloo. However, Mademoiselle made me rub out the doodles I drew in my French book, while FF didn't comment on the picture of Archimedes in his tub, exclaiming, 'Eureka – I haf found it!' although another teacher who saw it, reproved me with 'You rude girl!' I wanted to ask why it was rude, I wasn't aware of the double entendre.

Subjects I did not shine in: Sewing: I could never manage a thimble, and my efforts were always spotted with pinpricks of blood – we spent our first year making our cookery/science overalls. (These subjects were not studied until our third term.) I always felt it was unfair that the material, available in patterns of blue or orange, was given out by eye colour – thus, I didn't get my preferred blue, but the less popular orange, as it went with brown eyes. 'Me, too!' said Maggie, but she could at least sew beautifully.

AEC sighed over my feeble efforts in Maths. I could do mental arithmetic all right, but fractions, algebra and geometry were not my cup of tea. I couldn't comprehend why she had chosen two such different subjects in which to specialise. The only time I had a glimmering of hope maths-wise was when the Head Mistress, a lofty being of whom I was very nervous, took us for geometry one day and I suddenly realised that I knew what she was talking about... HM didn't give praise readily, she was the mistress of 'put down' but it was a pity she gave up teaching for administration.

Music lessons: these were taken around the piano in the Assembly hall. I soon learned to mime when we sang, because again I didn't fit into any category; I was demoted from the soprano section to the altos, and from there, to the 'drones.' I had always enjoyed singing, but now I was too self conscious to let any sound emerge. We had two girls with wonderful voices: an Irish girl called Marjorie, with black hair and bright blue eyes, who went on to sing at La Scala, Milan, and to join the Bach choir; a tall girl named Eileen rendered *Ave Maria* as I have never heard it before or since. Sadly she died very young. I can still 'hear' the three songs we practiced endlessly: *Linden Lea* (always performed at Prize-givings), *In Hans' old Mill* (his three black cats, searched the bins for the thieving rats – whisker and claw they crouched in the night, their five eyes shining green and bright...). My favourite was *Old Meg she was a Gipsy* (and lived upon the moors, her bed it was the brown heath turf and her house was out of doors...) I wished I could be like Meg and stare 'full hard against the moon'.

Then I discovered Disraeli. FF rushed into the classroom as usual, catching us chattering away. 'Question Number one', she cried imperiously, as she spread her books on the table. Desk lids flew up, paper and pencils located, but it wasn't until FF reached Question Number three, that we managed to scribble an answer. No-one ever received marks of ten out of ten for these quizzes on the previous lesson.

That day we were comparing nineteenth century prime ministers. Gladstone seemed very dull to me – who wanted a bag named after them? Disraeli, pictured as a young man, with Sephardic ringlets, dressed like a dandy, well, Queen Victoria obviously had a soft spot for him and I could instantly understand why.

When FF asked us to write an essay on a person in history we admired, naturally, I wrote about my hero, Disraeli. I put aside the 'book' I was writing in bed, early in the mornings (still my favourite time for writing) in purple ink.

I looked up D for Disraeli in the encyclopaedia at home. We had a whole set of these hefty tomes, and until now, David and I had only looked into a couple of them, mainly because it was a struggle to remove one from the shelf. We'd been fascinated by the diagrams of the human body, where you could 'lift' various organs to reveal further wonders beneath. So that's where the kidneys lurked, was it? And all those coils of 'sausages' were our intestines.. These 'pop-ups' were in colour: Disraeli was portrayed in black and white.

I knelt by my chair, with the book opened up at his name. Despite the dry language, I was mesmerised by the life story and achievements of this man.

I wasn't so impressed by his distinguished parliamentary career, as the fact that Disraeli was a writer, and much published. His novels were popular, sometimes satirical, but often romantic. Much later I discovered what the encyclopaedia didn't reveal: he was very attractive to women. However, his marriage to an older woman, the widow of a colleague, was known to be very happy. I also was touched by his devotion to his sister whom he called Sarianna, and the fact that he visited her grave often.

There was just one thing missing in Disraeli's life, in my opinion: he had no children with his devoted wife. I thought he must have been very lonely after she died, even though he became Lord Beaconsfield, and held many distinguished positions, including Prime Minister. So, in my essay I gave him a large family...

Long after I left school, and met FF once more, she told me she asked AEC: 'Did you know Disraeli had seven sons?' 'No! Did he?' 'Well, according to the gospel of St Sheila, he did!'

Writing essays were the highlight of my school life. Looking back over all the years I can see that I didn't quite fit in – I was not sporty, I was 'odd' in lots of ways. I had friends, who were important to me, but I was not a leader. I was sensitive, afraid of being laughed at when I used my imagination. AEC would read a selection of essays aloud to the class, asking, 'Well, who do you think wrote this?' I actually wished she wouldn't read mine, but she always did. I would sit there, feeling miserable, because the moment would surely come, when all heads would turn in my direction and the entire class would cry: 'Sheila!' AEC beamed proudly, but I wished the ground would swallow me up.

FOUR

Glycerine, Greens And Gristle

I have to admit that after the first excitement wore off, I wasn't too happy that my mother was so absorbed in the baby who'd joined our family. Molly looked after Jenny all day, while her mother was at work. Lily took charge of Jenny in the evenings, bathing and putting her to bed: David's room, which had also been wrecked by the bomb, was freshly decorated, and another single bed, the family cot and chest of drawers installed for Lily and the baby. Which meant that David had to continue to share my room. We had endless arguments around that time about our lack of privacy. 'Shush! You'll wake the baby,' we were admonished by Molly.

I think Jim realised I was feeling as I was, and had a tactful word with Molly, because she encouraged me to join her in cooking at the weekends. Like all mums, she was determined to provide treats for the family, better than bread buns from the bakers.

Low on margarine and lard? Add a tablespoon of liquid paraffin, or glycerine to the cake mix! When chemists realised why there was such a demand for such items, it was decreed sternly that these could only be used for the medicinal purpose for which they were intended. I recall the puzzling

wartime addition of Epsom salts to straw-
berry jam – 'for a moving effect!' joked a
popular WI speaker reminiscing about wartime economies, in the 60s.

Sweet treats? Pineapple chunks for a party?
Dice swede and add pineapple essence. We
had a gadget for making cream from the top
of the milk but it needed a little precious
butter and a spare hour or two to turn the
handle. Jam tarts? Bake pastry cases 'blind',
when cool, spoon in the jam. None wasted
'boiling over' in the oven. Best of all, when
we had a tin of golden syrup, we made
toffee, the way Molly had learned from her
grandmother. We added peppermint flavour-
ing to half the goo, looped rolls of almost set
toffee round the door knob and pulled
gently. When the toffee became paler, we
pulled one roll for longer, so that we had two
colours, the peppermint flavoured one
almost white and the other golden brown.
We twisted the strands together then snip-
ped the long strips with scissors into
humbugs. Much blissful sucking: Molly and

Lily were as eager to eat the sweets as we were. There was 'an extra ingredient', a hint of brass from the knob... Honeycomb was another favourite, which involved the use of bicarb to make it 'bubble'. Mint 'lumps' were made with powdered milk and a little icing sugar. These were rather sickly if you ate more than one.

We loved Molly's eggless fruit cake. Dried fruit was precious, but we used what we could get, like blocks of pre-war dates, adding flavour with ground ginger and mixed spice. This cake took very little margarine, brought to the boil with a cupful of sugar, flour and water in a saucepan, then a spoonful of bicarb, to enable the cake to rise, in the oven. 'Weevils!' Molly exclaimed once in dismay over the flour. Possibly some the grocer had produced from under the counter.

Puddings, savoury and sweet – semolina was used for milk puddings, in the absence of rice, likewise tapioca, known as frogs' spawn. The butcher sold kidneys encased in suet. This was removed and grated to add to the flour to make the topping for steak and kidney pud. This 'free' suet was saved for the Christmas pudding, too, along with dried apricots. I am ashamed to admit I once raided the apricot jar and the pudding was not quite so fruity that year... When lemons were unavailable, we drizzled baby's orange juice on our pancakes, courtesy of America and Jenny!

Maggie and I were allotted a plot in the school garden for growing vegetables. She was more knowledgeable than me, and I was far too squeamish about worms in her opinion. We had the most success with a packet of red cabbage seed. In triumph, in due course, I bore home an enormous cabbage. On Saturday, Molly and I pickled the shredded cabbage in vinegar. For supper that evening, we had our usual salad and we couldn't resist it, we opened the first jar and had a liberal helping of red cabbage! Molly wrote to tell Jim of our success and he answered wryly: 'This must be a record, pickling cabbage in the morning and eating it the same day!'

A girl named Mavis with a Welsh accent following evacuation to Wales, grew tender rhubarb. She picked it one lunch-time and put it in her desk and forgot to take it home. It was the day we broke up… Over the summer holiday the juice ran all over her books, and the acid almost destroyed them. This was a catastrophe for we often shared text books then. The same girl, I seem to think, put a parcel of fish, intended for the family supper, in her desk, and forgot that too. Following a warm weekend, the fish smelled to high heaven. Mavis was obviously a day-dreamer, too.

Desks were obviously vulnerable. A group of us decided to scrub our desks clean and re-polish them. The varnish disappeared, and so did we, when we heard a teacher approaching… I think she was alerted by the smell of lavender polish.

David grew tomatoes in our flower beds, and was very upset when a toddling Jenny picked 'the lovely little green apples.' They didn't even ripen on the windowsill.

We had an unusual plant in our school plot one day. We couldn't pull it up. It had quite a lot to do with school dinners, I'm afraid....

I feared lunch times almost as much as double Maths. (On typing this, I noticed that I hit the i key instead of the u in 'lunch' – maybe I should have left it uncorrected for 'linch'(lynch) might be more apt!) I sat with a different set of friends in the dining hall, Marjorie, the singer, Jean, who surely became an artist, Mavis, the rhubarb grower, and me. I had a new role now, encouraged by these girls, who all excelled in games, as a joker – they laughed at my prattle, bless 'em all. However, at the end of the table were the two who completed the six in our group. These were twins, identical, not small and appealing, but large and determined. I shall just refer to them as the twins! They actually had cherubic faces and wide, disarming grins. They were favourites of course with Miss GT, as they were athletic. They were also brilliant at maths. Anne liked them; later, she told me that the twins came from a strict religious family. I can think of them more charitably now, knowing that, maybe they were just letting off steam in picking on weaker brethren... They were bossy, exuberant teases rather than violent. (They actually went into caring professions when they left school.)

The twins appointed themselves in charge of our group, telling us when we could go up to the hatch and collect our dinner plates. There was a teacher in charge, usually Mademoiselle, who became tetchy when deprived of her cigarettes. 'Zut!' she cried in exasperation. Was that a swear word in French? We gasped in pretended shock. The rest of the staff wisely shunned the school lunches.

We were provided with a pre-lunch nibble – rusks, baked from stale bread. Whether these were to fill us up, or to preserve our teeth, I know not. The twins loved these rusks – they made good missiles, too, if one of the group wasn't paying attention. At first we were provided with jugs of water, but after several spills, these were banned. We also were deprived of the nice white table-cloths, which we had fun with after the meals, taking it in turn to pair up and shake out the crumbs, chanting 'Shadrak, Me-shak, Abednego,' as we folded the long linen neatly. So we ate on long trestle tables with plates on the bare wood.

The lack of linen revealed the horror beneath. On the trestle supports were bags of gristle, grease spotted. Like escaping prisoners-of-war, we concealed these on our persons when we rushed to freedom in the field, after lunch. Maggie didn't stay to lunch, she had permission (the gates were locked unless you had this) to go home to make sure her mother was all right. Despite the wheezing, little Maggie ran valiantly the short cut through the wooded area of the local park, scared stiff of who might jump out on her, to make a sandwich and a cup of tea for her mother and herself. Her mother, a sweet woman, had her two children late in her thirties, and I suppose she was suffering from depression, perhaps from the meno-pause. Maggie arrived back all out of puff just before the afternoon bell, to find me waiting, one day with a gristle bag. We buried it hastily in our Victory plot, and thought no more of it, until that giant, tough weed appeared. Maybe it was Jack's beanstalk!

Maggie wasn't the only one who had chores to perform for her mother during the lunch-break. Others, like Mavis, on occasion, had shopping to do, hence the fish in her desk. Chrissie had smaller siblings to collect from the nursery while her mother was at work, to take them to her grand-mother to look after. She was a clever girl, but these responsibilities (she was one of 18 children) meant she couldn't keep up with school work, and like several other nice girls, she left when she was fourteen, just before the school leaving age went up to fifteen. Another girl I really liked, Barbara, left then too, after her father was killed in action. Her mother later remarried a G.I. and Barbara and her sister had two small half-sisters.

Molly told me, 'You're one of the lucky ones having a good meal at midday. Maybe you won't be so fussy when I serve up something you don't like in future!'

The twins didn't worry about whether the food was edible or not. They had enormous appetites. Where all that extra energy came from, I suppose. I had trouble with the tough, dark greens served with nearly every meal. The horrible smell of them boiling on the stove wafted down the corridor to our classroom and made me gag I found it a real problem trying to force them down. We had to present empty plates for inspection at the end of the meal. We were often served with stringy mutton with lots of fat. Cooked beetroot was another problem for me: diced, purple and tasteless, not a bit like slices of beetroot in vinegar. We were given large mounds of lumpy mashed swede, too, which most of us disliked. When potatoes were in short supply, the creamy looking potato mash, we discovered was *Pom*, 'instant potato.' A favourite meal was corned-beef pie, until one day we had corned-mutton instead. The cooks did their best with unpromising ingredients. They tried hard with the puddings, although mostly it was semolina in various guises, sometimes coloured pink with cochineal. The best was chocolate pudding and white sauce. One day I was looking forward to this, while trying to munch the greens. A twin offered me a solution. 'Pass your greens to me, I'll eat 'em.' We watched in admiration as she forked them up, chewed and swallowed. 'Now, you've got to give me your pud – I've done you a favour, haven't I?' No disputing that.

Molly was right, I never complained about home cooking again.

We had bitterly cold winters during the

forties. Heating was rationed too. With a couple of like-minded friends I came in from the cold outside, creeping into the empty classroom to the bliss of sitting on a radiator, warming the atmosphere for the afternoon's lessons. We sat there quietly, absorbed in our reading books. FF patrolling the corridors startled us one day: 'What are you girls doing indoors – you should be outside getting lungfuls of fresh air!'

'My mum thinks I could get pneumonia...' one of us said.

'Rubbish! Don't be a ninny – move around, chase a ball, you'll soon warm up, and get off that radiator at once, you'll get piles!'

I was nudged, being urged to speak up. '*You* sit on it during lessons,' I dared to say.

She had an answer for that. 'I speak from painful experience – *I've* got them!' She couldn't resist a grin. Nor could we.

On another occasion, FF came into the classroom one day, and we almost didn't recognise her. She'd had a disastrous perm

– a shame, because she had such pretty wavy hair framing her attractive face. She was in a mood, not surprising, as she obviously couldn't get a comb through such an explosion of hair.

'What are you girls staring at? Go on, don't stop – I know I look a fright...' She paused, seeing our shocked faces. Suddenly she was laughing and we joined in with relief. What a sport she was. We made up romantic stories about her – surely she must have had a young man at one time, had he been killed in the war? She was politically minded – she'd told us about the Commonwealth party of which she was a member. Jim joked, 'Are you sure it isn't the Communist party?' 'Of course not, dad,' I said indignantly. Now I know that her mother was widowed, and left with two little girls to bring up on her own. Our FF had a fine intellect, she was given her chance to go to college. I imagine she looked after her mother after her sister married, once she became a teacher. Long after I left school I received letters from her: she was active in retirement, one message asked me to write to my local MP and demand the release of Nelson Mandela. She admired Frank Field – 'I don't always agree with his politics, but he is a good, fair man'.

Our secret huddles in the classroom on cold days were abruptly curtailed. The Bookworms were ambushed by the twins – my protests were muffled by parcel tape, but suddenly we became aware that the Head was in our midst. She demanded, 'Who did this to you?' I couldn't split on them. She hauled me off to her study for a lecture and dished out a hundred lines – 'hand them to me before you go home this evening.'

There was barely ten minutes to go before the bell. Miserably, I began to write. Tears welled in my eyes, it wasn't fair. A hand touched my shoulder, the twins stood there, looking at me. 'We'll help you,' they offered. We crowded onto my desk seat. They were experts in writing lines and had even tried tying two pens together to write two lines at a time. This time they just copied my handwriting and even though the Head's keen eye probably spotted the difference, she didn't comment, except for 'I hope you have learned your lesson.'

I certainly had, but best of all, the twins, if not my best friends, didn't bother me any more. I had earned their respect.

FIVE

Sealing Wax And Other Crafts

The Motts next door had been home for some time now. They had two children, too. Paula was a year older than me and attending the school I had not chosen. Perhaps this was just as well, for although Paula and I played together from an early age, we didn't have a lot in common. She had her school friends, I had mine. Her brother was much younger and still at primary school. In black and white snaps of the pre-war years, she wears the bridal veil (a net curtain) and carries the bunch of flowers, David is the bashful 'bridegroom', I am the bridesmaid, wearing wellington boots, and Paula's little brother is escaping the line-up in the Mott's garden in his pedal car. Paula was ever the one in charge of our little group.

Paula was considered to be more responsible than me, it was actually because she was capable of catching the bus somewhere and alighting at the right stop. I retained a short-sighted view on most things unless they were close-up, despite the new glasses. Paula and I went to the Applegarth dancing classes together, and she, being taller, was my partner in the Polka, which was our set piece. I got to wear the ballet dress which would have fitted her better, and she had to bow while I made a wobbly curtsey. I expect she felt she was saddled with me, but she was always polite and we never argued.

Our family always attended the local church both at home and in the country, but now we had no vicar in charge, just a succession of young curates, all awaiting call-up papers. David was in the choir, which made up most of the congregation. We had Children's Church with the Rev. Wilmshurst, who heard that I had been a regular reader in church since I was seven, and encouraged me to climb into the pulpit to read the lesson to the children. Then he asked me if I would be responsible for the CC log book. I tackled this with great enthusiasm, and wrote a glowing account of the Rev's wise words. I'm afraid I also described him as 'very handsome.' I should have heeded my Dad's opinion: 'Sheila, you let your pen run away with you!' I guess. The Rev grinned when he read my piece, but I was the one who blushed when asked to read it aloud to the other youngsters the next Sunday. When Rev. W departed, the CC folded, the choir continued, but that was all.

Paula, like Anne went to the Methodist

church. There was always a packed congregation, lots of happy singing and music. 'Why don't you come to chapel with me,' Anne suggested, 'All the young people sit in the gallery – no-one tells you to be quiet, and we can sing as loud as we like.'

Anne had been going to chapel on her own, whereas Paula went with her family. I decided to give it a try and Molly agreed, 'So long as you go to church, I don't mind which one.' David stuck with the choir, they had a short service at the old church when they met up. 'We sent toffees to each other in the collection plate.' That sounded tempting, but the choir was boys only.

I loved the atmosphere in the chapel gallery and the lusty hymn singing. They also had serious musical events, like Handel's *Messiah* to which folk flocked.

It was Paula who introduced me to the Guild, the Methodist youth club. There were so many activities on offer, it was hard to choose but I decided to take up a new handicraft which involved sealing wax... I also joined the drama club which I thoroughly enjoyed. Our coach had been a professional actress and she taught us how to project our voices without a microphone (I've been able to do this ever since) and in particular, I learned how to do a stage 'fall' without breaking any bones! She also encouraged me to sing and I regained my confidence in that respect.

Molly wasn't too sure about the sealing wax – this involved filling a little lamp with methylated spirit (which Paula said tasted quite nice!), lighting a wick, and holding the end of a stick of sealing wax in the flame… Highly dangerous, if hot wax dripped on your person. We cut out shapes from cardboard and made patterns from blobs of coloured wax. Then we pressed a little sharp tool (some of us used a manicure file) on the soft blob to mark petals or leaves – the design was often a rose, or other flower. A safety pin glued on the back of the cardboard, and you had a brooch. Molly wouldn't let me practice at home, with little

Jenny around, because of the unguarded flame from the lamp, but when I went round to Paula's, her mother had no qualms, because it was a quiet, sitting at the table activity, even though Mrs Mott was very house-proud and her children had to play with their toys in a pair of sheds, built by kindly Mr Mott, which were linked together by a roof over the entrance from the alleyway behind, so known as 'Peking.' I had a peek inside one of the sheds once: there was a huge Georgian dolls' house, fitted out with tiny furniture and figures. I wasn't allowed to touch, but was invited to watch while Paula changed a room around.

Paula had inherited two French dolls from her grandmother, exquisitely dressed, with real hair wigs. The dolls had porcelain faces with eyes which opened and shut, and rubber bodies, which surprised me. They smelled faintly of hot-water bottles. Again, I longed to handle one of these but had to wait while Paula brushed their hair into a new style. All I had was my old cherished teddy, Timothy Tapps, and he was almost bald after David shaved him with Jim's razor when he was about eight, assuring me, 'TT's fur will grow again...' Secretly, I thought I was luckier than Paula because we had a dog which could do tricks, like walking on her hind legs.

Mrs Mott's bedroom, in which we poked around when Mrs. Mott thought we were playing in Paula's room, was full of 1920's fashions kept from when Mrs M was a 'bright young thing.' Once Paula squirted some ancient perfume at me from a cut-glass bottle with a perished rubber ball: Mrs Mott sniffed the air suspiciously and gave me a look. She and Molly were not on Christian name terms until they were over seventy, and both widows.

I soon had a stockpile of brooches for Christmas presents. It made a change from the doyley holders (two doyleys in a parchment pocket: as we painted the doyleys, I shouldn't think the aunts fancied them under their cakes.) I had made too many writing cases from parchment, too, punching holes to hold the sides together, with a figure in a poke bonnet (no face needed) on the front. We split a pad of Basildon Bond paper, and added four envelopes. The Christmas before the sealing wax I asked Molly, 'Can I have some pieces of the firewood?' She agreed, but then wished she hadn't, for I painted little scenes on the wood with my new oil paints, and these remained so tacky to the touch, they were never given away.

David, meanwhile, continued with the manufacture of plastic wire bracelets. 'Much safer than sealing wax,' Molly advised me, but I couldn't pull the wire taut enough. The wire came in 'a tangle' from the electricity shop, in bright colours, and the bracelets were appreciated by our female relatives.

Maggie was a whiz at knitting and crochet, and she succeeded in teaching me not to do moss stitch instead of ribbing, and how to pick up dropped stitches, whereas my mother and aunt had given up on me.

Maggie invited me round to her house, which was very old and interesting – they had a gramophone with a horn, we put on records and danced about while clicking our needles and reciting 'Knit one, purl one, slip one, pass slipped stitch over...'

Her sweet mother made us cocoa, no milk and no sugar, 'good for you,' she said. Maggie's dad sang snatches of opera, he greeted me once at the door with a burst of 'Your tiny hand is frozen...' They were eccentric, and Maggie has inherited that charm. They made light of minor disasters – when rain came through their grandma's bedroom ceiling, the old lady called for an umbrella and sat up in bed to read the paper.

There was also a long garden, where you could pretend to be in the jungle, and rabbits in hutches. Maggie and her little sister Val cried when their pets ended up in the pot, and I felt for them. It was almost like being back in the country, making daisy chains and picking soft fruit from the currant bushes.

It was a strange time, the lull before the storm – getting back to more or less normality on the home front, at least as far as school was concerned, but listening on the wireless to news of the war raging in different parts of the world. We never missed *Children's Hour* and the classic serials. The *Daily Mirror*, Molly and Lily's choice, while Jim was away – when he was home he exclaimed: 'They've sent the wrong paper!' – of that time was very sparse, like all the papers, but the cartoons still kept going, though Jane became more saucy than she was pre-war. We saw newsreels in the Pav, but they were quite upbeat, even when showing weary soldiers in tin hats, smoking as they marched. We knew all the rousing songs and errand boys on bikes still whistled.

I went with Paula to a Knitting Squares meeting. We were the only young ones there. We were given small balls of wool, needles, told to cast on twenty stitches, and to knit squares for blankets – these were for use in air raid shelters. We missed out on an Anderson shelter in the garden at the beginning of the war, when we were away in Suffolk, but now we had an indoor shelter, a Morrison, which took up most of our front room. It was steel, as I recall and it made a good den for children.

Anne was busy with other sorts of craft at home, unknown to her mother, who was known as Jem, short for Jemima. She was an only child, like so many of our generation, and her parents were ambitious for their clever daughter. Anne came to school one day with little bags containing delicious, fizzy sherbet. She soon sold out at three pence a bag. We dipped into our bags, blissfully sucking our fingers. Like David's trade in white mice, the powers that be found out and stopped selling in the classroom. I begged for the secret of how to make it. 'Well,' she said, 'It all depends if your mum takes Andrews Liver Salts. No other kind will do. Mix with sugar... Simple, eh?' (Or were there other ingredients, if so, she didn't let on to me.) Jem wondered why the Andrews tin was empty, that was another snag. Anne went on, 'I shall have to think of something else...' I shouldn't be surprised if this made her determined to be a scientist. She eventually became a University Don which didn't surprise her friends.

Wartime children were encouraged to keep busy. We were always making something – mostly recycling things, as we do today once more. One day, we were told that a supply of new wool could be bought at school, no coupons, but only to dedicated knitters. Molly was all for it. 'You can make a school jumper,' she suggested. I made a face, I didn't want to knit in navy-blue wool.

AEC unpacked a large box in front of us. It was full of skeins of soft, brightly coloured wool, with evocative names – Spindleberry Pink, Coronation Gold, Sapphire Blue were my favourites. We were given simple patterns to knit jerseys with raglan sleeves. It was stipulated that these garments were for our own use.

I rushed home that night with my bag of wool, and before we had tea, Molly and I wound the first skein into a nice, fat ball. Well, she wound, and I held my arms wide with the skein looped over my wrists. She checked the pattern. 'Number twelve needles for the ribbing, then number nines. Bone or steel needles?' I chose the bone, though there was always the danger of them snapping mid-row when the knitting grew longer and heavier, but they were nicer, more pliable, to knit with than the rigid steel. I finished the rib before I went to bed that first knitting night. It stopped me from playing with the spills which we poked into the fire when Molly wasn't looking and whirled in our hands like sparklers.

I heard Molly say to Lily, 'Well, that was six shillings well spent...' I was proud that I was now an accomplished knitter. Thank you Maggie, for all your encouragement! My only regret is I never followed suit with sewing, but then I married John, who was quite capable of sewing on his buttons (and mine) and despite my ineptitude in that respect, our daughters (and sons) are all handy with a needle and thread (and sewing machine).

The sealing wax brooches were becoming more sophisticated, too. We discovered Glitter wax. This sparkled, as the name suggested. At Christmas our designs were holly and berries, mistletoe sprigs, the little blobs of red and white were very effective. We made all our Christmas cards and calendars. We made Dress-Dollies, small cardboard figures and designed tiny clothes for them. I also knitted a woolly hat and mitts in red with white bobbles so that Jenny would look like a mini-Santa on Christmas Day.

Of course, I never stopped reading and writing my stories – or dreaming... I also moved up to third place, next to Paula, in the tap-dancing troupe. We were booked for concerts in church halls, and even, though Molly would have disapproved had she been present, the local working men's club. Our 'turns' didn't stop the throwing of darts or the swilling of beer. I didn't mind we weren't paid, like David was for singing in the choir at weddings and funerals, because I got to wear a saucy pill-box hat and a red plastic costume, which you had to peel off at the end of the performance.

SIX

Dodging The Doodlebugs

The war was not over yet, even though we were now enjoying uninterrupted schooling. In the freezing January of 1944, Maggie, Anne and I queued outside a local sweet shop after school. The kindly, enterprising proprietors had hit on a winner: hot blackcurrant drinks. At 3d. a beaker, we were warmed up for the trudge home. The drink was fruity and delicious.

Although the evidence of the Battle of Britain was still all around us, we were not apprehensive like the adults, for we were confident the Allies would win the war. We listened to Vera Lynn singing *When the Lights Go On Again All over the World*, on the wireless, to Churchill's inspiring speeches, to *Workers' Playtime*, when we were having a day off school, and pups and kittens were named *Monty* after the General, who wore a beret, not unlike the majority of the juniors, which included me, in our school. Pudding basin velour was thankfully, out of favour, with wartime shortages.

The Mini-Blitz which began on 3rd February, took the general public by surprise. There were a number of night bombing raids on London. The ominous sound of the siren sent us scurrying to our shelter in the front room. Molly and Lily lugged the double mattress downstairs and manoeuvred it inside the steel cage.

Our shelter was intended for a family of

four. There were now six of us, when Jim was with us. He was about to transfer from Bath to Harrow 'for the duration of the war' which meant he would be able to live at home, although now he had given up the car he faced a lot of travelling each day to work. He was backwards and forwards at the moment, but as usual he didn't discuss his work. Once or twice a friend came with him, a nice chap in his forties, a bachelor, who obviously took a shine to Lily and Jenny. I guess Molly and Jim were doing a spot of matchmaking.

When we were all in the *Morrison* at the same time, we had to lie in a line across the width, rather than down the length of the structure. This was all right for the children, but the three adults wiggled their protruding feet ruefully, and hoped they'd have time to draw their knees up if disaster struck. Lily and I had Jenny between us, Molly was in the middle and David slept at the end, next to his dad. The only advantage of being squeezed together like this, was the shared warmth.

I said 'sleep' but this was very difficult. The boom of the guns, the relentless roar of the enemy planes – our torches flickered feebly as we attempted to read. It was reassuring to hear Jim talking to Molly, we didn't feel so fearful when he was with us. Lily didn't say much, she was a quiet girl and we were all fond of her. She cuddled her baby close and if Jenny cried, we sang nursery rhymes to lull her back to sleep.

After the *All Clear* we slept for a while, then returned to the daily routine. The bombing appeared to be confined to night time. David picked up shrapnel on his way to catch the school bus. Eventually he had a suitcase full. We imagined it would be worth a fortune one day… I walked to school as usual. The shelter there was opened and aired, and ready for emergencies, but I only recall a couple of false alarms. We carried our gas masks as well as our bulging satchels, but our Iron Rations had been consumed in 1940.

Paula and I had what we thought was a

good idea. We collected cigarette butts out of the gutter and painstakingly, and covertly, of course, removed the tobacco. When we had quite a wad, we left it to soak (and hopefully lose any germs) in the Motts water butt. Her father discovered it, and our parents gravely pointed out our foolishness. 'What did you intend to do with it?' asked Mrs Mott. We responded truthfully: 'Send it to the forces!' I think they were so relieved we hadn't intended to re-roll it and smoke it, no more was said. I shudder still when I think how Paula and I trailed behind a filthy old man and snatched up his smouldering cigarette end! I hope we washed our hands well.

The climax of the Mini Blitz came on 23rd of February, although the terror didn't end until 24th March, 1944: thirty-two boroughs reported incidents, including seventy-two people killed in a block of flats in the King's Road, Chelsea, when a direct hit was recorded.

In all there were one hundred and sixty

fatalities and serious injuries on that night. More than one thousand Londoners lost their lives during the Mini Blitz. Was this the final sting in the enemy 'tail'?

There was euphoria when D-day came at last on 6th June. The headlines in the *Mirror* took up the whole front page. The entire school cheered in Assembly. 'Wonderful news!' beamed the Head. We sang *'He Who would Valiant Be – Let Him Come Hither!'* Our pianist almost fell off her stool in her excitement at our fervour.

We were not aware then, of course, of the background to this historic event. We, and that probably includes most of the adult population who were not directly involved, only knew what we heard, from the wireless, read in the carefully edited newspaper articles or viewed in the newsreels in the cinema. We knew nothing of code-breaking, or secret intelligence, or the massive preparations taking place for the Normandy Landings. We were unaware of the gathering and special training of Allied troops in remote places in our island. We didn't know that the enemy had been fed false information and believed that the landings would be around the Pas de Calais where they had most reserves, while their troops were massed near Paris.

We did know that the Russians were fighting back and that the German Army was in retreat and we were told that the Allies had gained air superiority over western Europe. We learned that General Eisenhower, soon known to us all as 'Ike', was now The Supreme Allied Commander.

I can only relate how it seemed to me, as a twelve year old, at the time. John, who is two years older than me, realised what was happening more than I did. The boys at his school talked of spies and collaborators – of becoming old enough to join up, if the war lasted long enough... There was actually a reason for the rumours. The headmaster of the school, who had been evacuated with many of his pupils at the outbreak of war, was a compiler of crosswords in the *Telegraph*. Just before D-day he incorporated several of the code names used in the battle, like *Omaha* and *Utah*. Some of the boys at the school, it was said later, had 'fraternised' with G.I.s who were based nearby. The headmaster must have listened to their prattle and subconsciously remembered those names.

John, who'd joined the old-established school in Streatham, on his family's return from Scotland, where his father was involved with managing building runways for Lancaster bombers, was unaware of this at the time, or that the headmaster, whom he hadn't met then, was under suspicion. (John's and his sisters' memories of Scotland during the Forties, are woven into my novel for Hale, *The Spirit of Millie Mae*. The character of Barney is based on John.)

The summer of 1944 was an indifferent one – cold, wet and windy, but the events in June commenced when there was a sudden break in the stormy conditions. British and

American airborne divisions landed behind the beaches before dawn and at first light, British, Canadian and American troops moved on to the beach code-named as *Utah*, where the opposition were unable to stop their advance to contact the airborne divisions. The Americans were not so fortunate on *Omaha*, the other landing area, where they met a fierce barrage.

It was an exciting, if anxious time for those 'back home.' However, a new period of terror was about to begin for Londoners, who had already suffered and survived so much.

Before dawn on 13th June, 1944, the first V1, a small unmanned robot plane, a flying bomb, launched from Belgium, plummeted down and exploded in the capital. The railway bridge across Grove Road in Hackney was breached. This was a vital connection with Liverpool Street Station to East Anglia for the Great Eastern Railway.

From June until September, 1944, more

than 10,000 Doodlebugs (sometimes called Buzz Bombs, because of the noise they made) landed in Britain overall, but the main target was London. Our suburb was in the 'pathway' from the coast. Croydon became known as 'Bomb Alley.'

Londoners carried on despite spending sleepless nights 'under the stairs.' Milkmen and postman climbed over rubble as they had during the Blitz, to deliver milk and letters.

In our shelter in the front room, a little voice piped up: 'Them damn Doodle-bug-gers!' For a moment there was a shocked silence: where on earth had young Jenny heard those words? Swearing was taboo in our house. Then, if the shelter hadn't been of such rigid construction, it would have rocked with our laughter.

Lily went to the factory in the morning, and Molly poked the sheets in the steaming copper in the kitchen. Jenny 'read' to Dinkie the dog. David and I went our separate ways to school. I'm sure Molly was fearful for our safety, for the Doodlebugs arrived 'out of the blue' at any time, day or night, but we were expected to attend classes, if possible.

The R.A.F. didn't let us down. When the Doodlebugs arrived our side of the Channel, the pilots of Spitfire, Mosquito and Mustang planes were waiting to tip the glider wings and to turn them back, while those which got through were bombarded by anti-aircraft guns.

I was wending my way along the high street, unaccompanied, when I became aware of the now-familiar buzz. The Doodlebugs flew low at around 350 miles per hour and were clearly visible, if you looked up. I quickened my pace, but it appeared to be following me – in mounting panic I looked vainly for shelter. The shops were still shuttered, no-one was about. Then the buzz abruptly 'cut out' – the Doodlebug was diving. I flung myself down on the pavement, hands over my ears. If I hear the explosion, I told myself, it hasn't landed here. A few moments later came the great blast. Fearfully, I got up on my knees and opened my eyes. Way up the road I saw a crater, with smoke and flames. I heard the fire engine bell, and people were already gathered with stirrup pumps.

Shaking all over, I stumbled on to school. 'Why didn't you come home?' Molly asked me that evening.

'I don't know,' I said.

I can't remember if the teachers questioned me about my dishevelled appearance. The rest of that day, until I somehow managed to get home, is a blank.

I'm not sure if school broke up early for the summer holidays because of the Doodlebug menace, or if our parents decided to send David and I back to Suffolk to our everwelcoming family there for a break.

Molly decided not to join us there for a time, because Jim was now working in Harrow full-time. She also felt responsible for Lily and Jenny. Lily couldn't leave the factory and she was needed to look after

Jenny all day.

David and I took Dinkie with us, and were old enough now to help with carrying our luggage. We stood on Liverpool Street Station, the train had came alongside, and even as doors opened, the siren wailed. Porters ran up and down the platform slamming doors and making sure windows were closed. We didn't have time to say goodbye properly to Jim. Distressed, we waved frantically at him from the corridor of the train, not having yet found seats.

Even through all the station cacophony we heard the ominous sound of the Doodlebug, right overhead.

'Dad!' we shouted, even though we realised he couldn't hear us. We spotted him hurrying away among a crowd of people, then they all disappeared into a waiting room. The buzz stopped abruptly. We heard the explosion, as the train gathered steam.

David held on to my arm, and I clutched the dog's lead. 'It's all right,' he tried to convince me, 'come on, they've made room for

91

us in the carriage.' He paused then added unsteadily, 'It went over the station, I'm sure...'

Our uncle met us at the other end. We climbed aboard his lorry and were soon back at the cottage to a warm welcome from Dolly, Auntie Rum, Jassy, now six years old, and her baby brother, red-haired like his mother and sister.

Telegrams were sent between Suffolk and Surrey. Ours said simply, *'Arrived safely, love to you all'* and Molly's read, *'Dad all right, love from us. Mum.'*

Come September, we travelled back home. The V1 threat had dwindled, but shortly there was another horror to contend with, the V2. This was a ballistic missile, aimed mainly at London during the Autumn and Winter of 1944. The first V2 fell in Greenwich, the second in Epping. They travelled faster than the speed of sound, so there was no warning: survivors were only aware of a sonic boom after the crash. Half the V2s failed to reach the capital, but caused havoc in the suburbs. South and East London took the brunt of the new wave of bombing.

We went to school, we went to work, we spent our days at school often in the shelter, and at night we slept in the Morrison. Life had to go on, you see. We stoutly believed that the end of the war was in sight.

SEVEN

All Those Begats And Shakespeare Too.

When our school had an influx of pupils, due to the return of the evacuees, for a term or two our class moved temporarily to the Science lab. This was designated our form room, we met there for registration with AEC and had the first lesson of the day with her there after Assembly, then moved around the school to vacant classrooms, when the usual occupants were elsewhere, like the art room, domestic science block or gym. I usually just followed on the end of the crocodile, confident I would then arrive at the right place at the right time.

The mention of *Pilgrim's Progress* evokes the smell of the lab, of substances used in experiments. We moved aside the Bunsen burners, test tubes, on slab like tables which bore the marks of spills and burns, and opened our books.

I needed to pay attention, not to turn the pages too far ahead while AEC read aloud to us, because it was very likely that she would pause, then ask 'Who would like to read the next chapter to us?' When no immediate response was forthcoming, she would say brightly: 'Sheila?'

Later, there was an unexpected reprieve for those who were keener on sport than religious instruction. For some time in the gym we had been learning to swim – no water in sight: it was called Land Drill. I actually enjoyed this and lying on my front on a form, I performed a credible breast stroke. Miss GT was so impressed, she called the rest of the gymnasts over to watch me in action.

Molly gave me the written permission needed to join a weekly swimming class at the Municipal Baths. These had recently reopened, and local schools were keen to take advantage of this out of school activity.

The water was chilly, the smell of chlorine was powerful, there was much jostling in the changing rooms. The noise was horrific, the tiles slippery and we were told we would never make swimmers if we couldn't duck our heads under water, as we shivered in the shallow end. Miss GT pounded up and down calling encouragement, 'Hold your noses, you duffers!' but I failed dismally to go under water even for a few seconds. I never got a chance to show off my breast stroke, anyway, I daren't take my feet off the bottom of the bath, and I couldn't believe the assurance, 'You'll float!'

How I wished I was back among the

Bunsen burners and reading aloud.

In the end I was unexpectedly released from purgatory and shame when the swimmers (and one non-swimmer) were lined up ready to leave the Baths one morning. We were waiting for Miss GT to join us and blow her whistle for the 'Off.'

'Look!' pointed one of the twins (who were of course already powerful swimmers). We crowded to the edge of the baths to watch a diver on the springboard. A solitary male among all the adolescent girls present! He was, we learned later, a soldier on leave, a keen swimmer.

I was so entranced by this performance, I failed to notice that the rest of our team had melted away at the sound of the whistle… A hand gripped my shoulder. I was summarily banned from the swimming lessons, but I can't say I was sorry. AEC was sympathetic and listened to my version of events. I was back with the *Pilgrim's Progress* and although I have always regretted not being able to swim, I was much happier. Even though I had to put up with a painful verruca on the ball of my foot, which I 'caught' at the swimming baths!

We were back in a regular classroom when we read the bible from beginning to end. I was apparently the only one interested in reading aloud in R.E. I projected my voice to good effect: All those 'begats' – I soon learned that if you could make dull phrases sound interesting, the class would listen. I wasn't really aware of it then, but I had a captive audience, and have been a performer, ever since.

I expect some of my classmates considered I was becoming a show-off, but looking back, I was only hoping to be liked, while masking the fact I actually felt inadequate beside confident, popular Big Girls who excelled at sport and whom the rest of us admired. I'm sure I was not alone in this.

There were some very nice, upright girls in our class. Marion and Marian, they spelt their name slightly differently, were admired by their fellows and teachers alike. They were 'girls to be trusted', and Marion with an 'o' was my house captain. I tried hard not to let Marion and the green team down. When I was feeling poorly one day and was too bilious to eat my lunch, Marion found me in the cloakroom, and helped me clean myself up. Then she washed her comb under the tap, and gently tidied my hair. I felt much better after her ministrations. Marian was extremely artistic, she still produces beautiful paintings of plants and flowers. These days, she sets up her easel on her balcony overlooking the sea.

Years after we left school, I met them both, along with other school friends, at an Old Girls' reunion organised by Di, who like me became a writer, by then, she was President of the Romantic Novelists Association, a post she still admirably fills. Anne was there too, recently retired from an illustrious career, and now working tirelessly in her local community. It was good to see Eileen and Vivien after so many years: Eileen had possessed a lovely evening dress, given to her by a glamorous aunt, and I had not been the only one to borrow it for a formal dinner and dance when we were seventeen or eighteen! Vivien had a very special place in AEC's affections, having survived a serious accident when we were still juniors at the school. It was great to see her, tall and beautiful, fit and well. I wished Maggie had been there, but like some others she felt too much time had elapsed.

Di produced our final year school photograph. She was now sophisticated and glamorous, a top editor with a prominent publisher, but there we both were, sixteen, going on seventeen, like the song, side by side in the front row, looking bashful. I wear my (old) school tie. As I failed to knot it correctly when I was eleven, Molly inserted elastic at the back, so I could slip it easily over my head after gym. She could always find a solution to problems, my mum. She'd done the same with my Brownie scarf when I couldn't to tie a reef knot, though I was only seven then.

I recognised Marion and Marian right away. They had lived up to their early promise and it was good to see them again. All of us who met that day had experienced adversity in one way or another, but come through, the stronger for it. FF joined us at several of these meetings, and she remarked that we must have been a 'good vintage year' because so many of us had succeeded in life. We wondered what had happened to some of the less conventional girls – Rosemary, for instance, who had the exotic (then) middle name of Scarlett, and who sent AEC a card from Egypt, a year after she left our class...

I was never monitor material – though I was made responsible for a girl who was prescribed a daily dose of cod liver oil and malt following our first Medical. She tried hard but she just couldn't swallow the required tablespoonful. I was supposed to encourage her to open her mouth and see that it all went down her throat. She cried so much at her first attempt, 'I can't do it! I just can't! I'll bring it all up again!' that I offered nobly (because I disliked it, too) to take the dose for her. We were alone in the Domestic Science kitchen, where the large jar was kept in a cupboard. I took a deep breath and did the deed. I was literally stuck with this thereafter, and the girl who needed the supplement was duly pronounced, 'Much improved.' I don't think she felt guilty, but I certainly did.

I was once called a monitor – by the Head, no less. I'd been spotted whispering to Maggie during a lesson, and was told to stand outside in the corridor 'until you can control yourself.' This was a mild punishment, but the chatterer, of course, felt conspicuous, and apprehensive who might pass by...

That particular afternoon, I heard footsteps and voices in the corridor which led off the one where I stood. I recognised the Head's bell-like tones. In a panic, because I could tell they were headed my way, I nipped into the adjacent store. Would I be spotted? I bent over a pile of text books, as if I had just put them down.

The Head stood in the doorway, after flicking on the switch. I hadn't thought to turn the light on. She spoke to the accompanying school inspectors: 'And this is one of our young monitors ...' I looked up and saw the glint in her eye. She knew, and I knew, I was nothing of the sort. She was human, after all!

Miss C was a handsome woman, with auburn hair wound round her head, not plaited, but twisted. She was the niece of the original head mistress, and was proud to be carrying on the family tradition. She would point out the names on the impressive Honours board, in the Assembly Hall. She knew what these special girls had achieved in later life. Among them was 'dear Peggy Ashcroft, who is a famous actress.' I wished Peggy was still my age and at the school, for I would have loved to know her.

Whenever I came face to face with Miss C, my knees turned to jelly. She knew the name of every girl in the school. She always managed to temper praise with a rebuke in my experience. Many years later I received a letter from her, after she read of a writing achievement. 'You have a gift, I do hope you use it, Sheila.' Oh, I try, Miss C, I do. Thank you for remembering me. I shall never forget you.

Only once did we perform Shakespeare on stage – Anne was producer, and she cast me as Henry V's Queen. I had to tell her I didn't feel I looked the part. I could project my voice yes, but I didn't well, have the figure for it. In a couple of years that would change, but then I felt I would be under-developed for ever... Rosemary, she who went off to Egypt and was never heard of again (by us anyway), stepped into my shoes. I took on several roles that others spurned as too small. I was in my element, playing old and young, male and female, and employing different voices. Unfortunately, the play, which was performed after school hours, was far too long, and some of the audience sneaked out before we reached the final act. Anne had put her all into the production, and the cast felt for her, and her disappointment.

Palgrave's Golden Treasury: those wonderful poems have remained in my memory always. Like most of my friends, and my husband, I often quote much loved lines. Keats and Shelley were my favourite poets.

Some of the books we studied – we began with *The Water Babies* – and learned the message behind it, the exploitation of child labour. *Jane Eyre*, *Pride and Prejudice*, and *The Thirty-nine Steps*, all the classics were enjoyed in turn, due to AEC's presentation and skilful interpretation. I found Sir Walter Scott somewhat indigestible – the plots were good, the scenery marvellous, but they were too wordy. I admit to skipping some of this author's pages, not compulsively turning them... *Lorna Doone* caught my imagination *Travels with A Donkey*, Robert Louis Stevenson, now there was a story-spinner after my own heart. I didn't really relate to Dickens during my school days, but when I saw the cinema versions (often with John Mills) and later enjoyed the serialisations on TV, I went back to the books, which pleased my father, for Dickens was his favourite author.

As for William Shakespeare – we read aloud one of his plays in class each term – I was in my element, thanks to AEC casting me, as Bottom, Shylock (much rubbing of hands and oily tones) and Lady Macbeth! Ditto the wringing of hands but with a Scottish accent. In the latter, when we reached the more eloquent speeches, AEC would invariably say: 'We'll leave out the next two pages, I think...' But I did get in 'Out damned spot' and gave it my all. Naturally, the forbidden pages were read with much interest by the rest of the class!

A few years later I went with John to Theatre in the Round and saw the great Bernard Miles in the title role. We discovered that we had both been taken by our schools to see the film of Henry V with Laurence Olivier – we may even have been in the audience at the same time, but we didn't meet then...

A highlight of those middle school years was the Elizabethan Week – in which every single pupil was involved. Our class chose to do the art work. Maggie made tiny boots and shoes with scraps of leather – I do hope these are preserved somewhere. Others made costumes. Doublet and hose, paper ruffs. Who made the lovely miniature four-poster bed? With linen and bedspread, too. Wisely, I opted to illustrate the Globe theatre. Well, it was a pen and ink drawing, but I gave it a 'wash' of pale green. Visitors were invited at the end of the week to view the displays – all subjects were covered, like maths, science and sport. This event was a great success and much reported in the local press.

I like to think that William Shakespeare would have approved. I'm not so sure about Queen Elizabeth the First. She had an aloof expression in her portrait, whereas Sir Walter Raleigh had a twinkle in his eye...

Our bright young Art teacher was leaving us, for pastures new – an art college. Some of us, including me, were asked if we would like to transfer there with her. I rushed home to tell Molly the exciting news. 'Certainly not!' she cried. 'You can do all the drawing you like at home – you've got exams to pass, my girl!'

I consoled myself with the thought that I would illustrate my books myself, in the future. Alas, no-one has ever suggested that I should. However, two of our daughters are artists – and teachers – though I think their talent in that respect comes from their father, rather than me. Some of the grand-children have inherited this gene too, in fact all our children are creative in one way or another. As for writing, I have hopes!

EIGHT

Dancing In The Street

How can I describe the relief and sheer exuberance of VE Day, which was celebrated on May 8th, 1945? The *Mirror* proclaimed: *It's Over In the West!* followed by: *London has Joy Night.* Winston Churchill broadcast to the nation from No. 10. Huge crowds gathered outside Buckingham Palace and cheered the Royal Family when they appeared on the balcony. The King's speech was relayed to the crowd.

We heard that effigies of Hitler burned on bonfires, that long-hoarded fireworks exploded all over the country, maybe there were a few damp squibs, but who cared? In our own high street, there was dancing ... the trams were at a standstill. Singing, too –

some of it sentimental but some ribald. *'Show me the way to go home,'* was traditional, but *'Roll Me Over in the Clover,'* I knew was rude. The church bells pealed and we found standing room only when we went along to the special thanksgiving service at midnight. Lights blazed everywhere, in homes and shopping parades.

I wrote about this time in *The Family From Number Five*. It was based on personal experience – but because of my own mixed emotions at the time, I was thirteen, remember and easily embarrassed by adults when they behaved like adolescents themselves. It is better, I think, to quote from my story:

Glory and Don walked along together. She was well aware of his sidelong glances. She was pleased she was wearing the new blue skirt Mirry (her mum) had finished this morning, a dirndl, like Miss Fizzbang's, a style her mum agreed was economical with material. It went well with the Hungarian blouse Grandma had brought home in triumph from a jumble sale – fine muslin, brightly embroidered yoke, drawstring neck and short, puffed sleeves. A bit see-through her mum said doubtfully, so she must hitch up the straps of her petticoat to conceal her cleavage. She was proudest of her Clark's sandals: with cross over straps in brown leather leaving her toes bare: another sixpenny jumble prize. She still wore her hair short, the bubble cut was becoming popular now, so she was ahead of fashion.

The Spa gardens were crowded with people: children played hide-and-seek around the rose bushes and the men queued patiently for drinks. Junie eyed the local boys, dripping with Brylcreem, seemingly unaware of her proximity. Mirry and Laura (Junie and Don's mum) were still talking animatedly, only Bar (Mirry's sister) sat quietly with the older ladies. Glory and Don ostensibly kept watch on Boo and Robin, while sitting on the grass, making daisy chains to amuse their charges.

'You've got a cherryade moustache,' Don told her.

'Better than pickled onion breath,' she retorted.

'They went down well, with that spam roll,' he

said, 'disguised the taste of marge – I hate marge! When I get married, I shall order only butter in my house!'

'If we ever get rid of rationing, Don.'

He looked at her in surprise. 'The war's over, isn't it? Surely rationing will end soon?'

'How can it? The countries we used to import from are struggling to survive – people are starving – it will take years for the world to recover from this war.'

'You're very knowledgeable, Glory! I didn't think girls were interested in politics. Oh, I know my mum says you're too clever by half–'

'Oh, does she! That drop of cider has loosened your tongue, I see, Donald Sims. What a cheek!' But she smiled at him, because it was nice to be thought clever, even by half.

Maybe it was the illicit glass of cider, which he hadn't expected to get, although he'd grandly requested it, mainly to impress Glory, when his dad asked for their orders, but Don suddenly saw her in a fresh light. She was a pretty girl, the sort boys would fight over, and he'd known her all his life, so he was in with a good chance...

111

'Like to come to the Pictures this weekend?' he asked casually. 'There's an Edward G. Robinson film.'

Glory didn't like gangster films, she took after Mirry for musicals and love stories, with spunky heroines, of course. But – she'd actually been asked out on a date! Her very first. 'Don't see why not,' she agreed casually, then, 'where have those two terrors got to, Don? We'd better go and look.' As she jumped to her feet, he noticed that she had painted her toenails with pink varnish, and that her long legs were shapely and golden from the sun.

Down the hill they rolled the pickled onions, gathering dust, with the smaller children shrieking their delight as Mirry and Laura continued to let their hair down. The older children, in an agony of embarrassment, kept well to the rear this time, stony-faced. The rest of the party displayed tolerance. Actually, Fred (Glory's dad) could hardly believe his eyes there was Mirry, retrieving her battered onion from the gutter and Laura singing out: 'I've won!

Loser gets to eat the champion onion!'

Boo and Robin were doing a jig of excitement.

'No fear!' Mirry replied, 'Anyway, we haven't quite reached the bottom of the hill...' and she bowled her onion past Laura's, where it hit the lamp post and smashed to pieces.

'Draw!' Jim said hastily. 'Now sober up you two, those three at the back think you've gone quite mad!'

This was the first and last time I ever saw my mum tipsy – after two glasses of gin and lime! Alcohol was rationed too... And I shall never forget the Great Pickled Onion Race – ever!

There was one last hurdle to overcome, and it was on a visit to the cinema that Maggie and I saw the terrible effects of the Atomic bomb in full colour. I can still conjure up in my mind's eye that great mushroom cloud and how disturbing it was. VJ day followed: we were staying with Dolly and family in Suffolk for the summer holiday. Beacons were lit along the coast line and there was a celebration fete in the village and country dancing on the grass.

It was the summer our little dog wriggled through the garden hedge into the field beyond and met up with the school care-taker's wire-haired ancient terrier – my cousin Laura, who was engaged to an American airman then serving in the Pacific, and visiting for the weekend, jumped the hedge and brought Dinkie back, but it was too late: a couple of months later, little Dinkie gave birth to six big pups. It was exciting at the time, but she was too small to cope. I was heartbroken, when the vet told us she had hysteria, and must be put down. Molly took on the pups, who had to be weaned, of course, at three weeks old – they all survived, but we decided not to keep any of them. I declared: 'There will *never* be another dog I will love like Dinkie,' but, thankfully, in time, there was...

There were other changes: Lily married Bob, Jim's friend, in Bath, where they settled with Jenny. This was a happy outcome for them, but I know Molly missed the baby. We were getting back to normal as a family unit at last. I had my bedroom to myself, so did David, and he helped Molly plan a lovely surprise for me for my birthday. Molly was always a dab hand with a distemper brush and at hanging wallpaper. The latter wasn't readily available, so my bedroom walls were painted pink and butterflies, cut from a pattern book, fluttered in each corner. The ceiling was painted blue and David cut silver stars from milk bottle tops and stuck these on. So I got my wish, I was like Old Meg in the song, looking up at the heavens above, but comfortable on my feather mattress! My friends were most impressed.

This was a new chapter in school life, too. There were outings to London, to exhibitions like *Britain Can Make It*, to museums and art galleries, a trip down the Thames on a boat, with AEC and FF – enlivened by the fact that some girls (the twins and friends?) had gone aboard the wrong Tube train, and we all had to wait on the platform for their return. Later, there were holidays in Walmer, with the school. Maggie went on one of these but her report put me off joining them the following year! I enjoyed her descriptions of teachers in steel curlers at breakfast, but not lights out and no talking, at 8 o'clock!

FF planned a historical walk for the third form. One Saturday Maggie and I and several others caught the bus to Croydon, and followed a route to Westerham, to see General Wolfe's statue, and Winston Churchill's country home. We went in pairs, in a straggly crocodile (the twins I expect, were in the lead), looking at our instructions and wondering when we could open our gas mask cases and take out our packed lunch. But this was not permissible until we reached our destination, and met up with FF (who hadn't come on foot!).

Maggie and I were in a group of six, including another Marion, whose father had just been demobbed. As we sat on a patch of grass opposite General Wolfe, who naturally ignored us, to eat our spam sandwiches, Marion casually produced a banana. She proceeded to slice it into six portions and generously shared this treat, brought home by her dad, with us. Just a mouthful each, but we felt the luckiest girls on the walk! We wrote the essays expected of us, later, and I think the banana was the most memorable part of the exercise.

The yearly examinations were very serious affairs. Because we sat in double desks, classes were intermingled, so there could be no chance of cribbing. This meant that a third former could be sitting next to a first former. The sixth form, being lofty individuals, were by themselves in the hall. The only sounds you could hear during exams were the rustling of paper and the scratching of pens. Later, would come the suspense of results. I always kept my head down during the maths call. I knew it wasn't worth raising my gaze until the forties were reached, and that was being hopeful. Thank goodness for

English Lit., English Language, History and Art – I could breathe again then.

Once, the whole school sat a special examination. It was one I really enjoyed, because we were only told 'It is General Knowledge.' We heard no more for ages, and forgot about it.

The Head came unexpectedly into our classroom one day. We rose obediently and wished her Good Morning, then resumed our seats. Her piercing gaze swept across our faces. Then I realised she was looking at me. There was an audible sigh of relief from my classmates. AEC smiled encouragingly at me, from the front of the class, but I was blushing, all over it seems. What had I done wrong? I frantically went through any very minor misdemeanours in my mind. I swallowed convulsively.

Miss C continued to regard me thought-fully. 'Sheila?'

'Yes...' I managed at last.

She tapped a sheet of paper she held. 'You will recall the unusual test you all performed some time ago?'

'Yes,' chorused the rest of the class.

'We didn't enlighten you at the time, but this test was given in all schools in the country. Each school has received an individual report. The Education Department wanted to know if pupils were reaching their full potential. This is an I.Q. test – of intelligence.'

We were all trying to take this in. I was also wondering, 'Why me?'

'You, Sheila Langley – stand up, so we can all see you – have scored top marks in this school. I am pleased to report that the Head Girl came second...'

The Head Girl – how on earth could I have gained more marks than that brilliant girl, of whom we were all in awe? Or even Anne, who was always top of the class, sometimes tying with Myra, another mathematical and scientific minded girl. (Anne admitted later that she found the paper 'boring'.)

While I stood there, scarlet and silent, Miss C added the expected 'put you down.'

'Now we know what you are capable of, Sheila, we shall expect *much* more of you.' Then she swept out.

The class clapped, I sat down and AEC said kindly, 'Well done, Sheila. Your parents will be proud of you.' But I had already decided I couldn't tell them because they might well agree with Miss C! After all, they had queried a remark on my last report which stated, 'Sheila is not steady enough'. Later I enlightened them sheepishly about that: 'The teacher was Miss Barker, she'd long been retired, but she helped out in an emergency. We thought of Eric Barker, and his catch phrase, on the wireless. 'Steady Barker!' When she shouted, 'Steady, girls, steady!' we murmured that in return. She couldn't hear us, fortunately.'

Jim told me: 'That wasn't very kind.' And it wasn't, was it? I'd felt ashamed when she stopped me in the corridor, the day she left, and told me, 'I shall miss your lovely smile.'

Looking back, others had their problems, like me. Maggie struggled gamely with her asthma, but never complained: our friend Pat stammered badly. The amazing thing in her case was that when asked to read aloud, she was transformed – she had a lovely voice. Pat emigrated to Australia soon after we left school – I wonder if she became an actress? For my part, I became increasingly myopic, prescriptions were not changed often enough: at times I was squinting at the board, even from the front row. I also suffered bilious attacks as Molly termed them, which meant time off school – I then had to attempt 'catch-up.' This developed into migraine. I was on a long waiting list for a tonsillectomy. Molly always suspected I had a weak heart, because I often turned 'blue' as a baby, but the leaking valve was not discovered until I was in my fifties!

I come from a fair-skinned, often combined with red or fair hair, family, and all the females blushed: I was sometimes thought guilty of something which I knew nothing about – but when a teacher demanded:

'Who did this?' I flushed from head to toe – or that's what if felt like. Molly couldn't understand why I spent so much time in my room, reading and writing, instead of wanting to go out with my friends. I was nothing like my extrovert mother at my age. From what she said, I gathered that teenage tantrums and hormones then, were ignored!

David, on the other hand, was certainly out and about – very involved with a new youth club and sport, including long-distance running: he loved playing table tennis and in later in life became a national coach. He persuaded me to join the club, which was for teenagers upwards, unlike the Guild, and although reluctant at first, I shortly found myself editress (as it was termed then) of the club magazine. Here I was in my element, although not so keen on typing the stencils on an antiquated typewriter where the keys flew up and stuck firmly in mid air, or applying sticky red correction fluid to my many mistakes. Contributions from the club representatives were often scribbled scrawls, and one from I.K. had Jim exclaim: 'What does the I stand for – illiterate?!' I'm afraid I was soon writing the whole magazine under different guises, which I didn't mind at all... In fact the local paper congratulated one of these fake correspondents for an excellent report - I got to meet the cub reporter, one Gerald Williams (you may have heard of him!) who took me out for coffee. As he reported on Crystal Palace football club my brother was keen to meet him, being a fan, and asked me if I would let him go in my place! I refused naturally!

Anyway, I was about to embark on a social life, much to Molly's relief, But that's another chapter.

NINE

Donkeys, John Bull And Tangos

Our first seaside holiday for seven years was taken the year after the war ended. We shared a bungalow with Dolly, Russ, Jassy and young Nick. Jaywick, near Clacton was the choice, being roughly half-way between our two homes. There was still barbed wire to be seen on beaches, and some places were sign-posted out of bounds due to danger from unexploded mines or because the beaches had been used by the army on manoeuvres.

David joined us both weekends, for he had not long been in his first job in a London stockbrokers. He said running came in useful there! Whit week, at the end of May was chosen, and we were lucky, for there was a heatwave.

My cousin Laura, a GI Bride, now in the States, sent me a parcel of clothes, most as good as new. I had worn hand-me-downs and make-overs for so long, I could hardly believe my luck! Laura was a tiny girl, and later her offerings, alas, were too tight (she must have been a size 8), but I made the most of my new wardrobe while it fitted! Among the items was a super swim suit. Having worn an old, ruched costume of Molly's at the swimming baths, I was disappointed that this one was rather tight round the middle. Molly had an inspiration – she cut it at the waist, and I had a two-piece! 'You look like a film star,' she told me. Poor Jassy had to make do with a bathing suit knitted in stripes by me, which sagged when it got wet. I don't think she minded, as she was only eight, but she was good company for me, as I was a rather immature fourteen year old, like most of my friends. We were the first generation not to go out to work at an early age – our parents seemed determined to keep us innocent and to enjoy a belated childhood which up to now had been restricted by the war.

The 'bungalow town' was a great sprawl, and some of the holiday lets were quite a way from the beach. It was nothing like the places we had stayed in pre-war Norfolk, with countryside all round and cliff paths to descend to soft, clean sand and sparkling sea – but we soon overcame our initial disappointment, for now I was considered the responsible one, and Jassy and I were allowed to go off on our own sometimes, like first thing in the morning, to collect newspapers and milk.

The bungalow was very basic, with three bedrooms and a sofa bed in the living room for David, but Molly and Dolly were impressed with the pull-down ironing board – I recall them ironing their cotton dresses while clad in their petticoats because it was so hot. Jim and Russ riled them by snatches of *'Marta (Martyr!), Rambling Rose of the Wild Woods'*, but they never joined us on the beach until lunch-time. Actually, I think they enjoyed time on their own together.

We didn't have a dog then, but we had a tabby cat, called Tikki. We took him on holiday with us, and he didn't mind being on a puppy lead and collar, and was agreeable to being transported in a basket on the train. He was really Jim's pet, and known to him as 'The Old Gentleman.' 'Oh,' he said, when the cat was curled up on his lap on winter evenings, and Molly looked meaningfully at the empty coal bucket at home, 'I'm afraid I can't disturb The Old Gentleman.' She retorted: 'I can!' and she did.

Jassy and I were in charge of Brandy, a golden cocker spaniel, but not so keen on her little brother tagging along with us.

We discarded our shoes on the first day of the holiday, and didn't put them on again until we went home at the end of the week. It was fine on the beach, but we hobbled sometimes up the road, particularly if we trod in something nasty.

Ice-cream was still a real treat. Back home, Paula and I had recently left the Applegarth dancing school, and now we went to Croydon to spend our pocket money on Saturday mornings. Our favourite shop was Kennards store, which always seemed like a covered market place, bustling, with many departments and an overriding smell from *Pets Corner*, down in the basement area, which led out to Surrey Street Market. There were sweet puppies in runs, which I lingered over, and parrots and other exotic birds on perches, calling out 'Hello!' or squawking loudly. The pups were of indeterminate breeds, and I'd be warned not to buy one by my mother. As they were five shillings, this was unlikely, for I had other things to spend my money on. This included ice-cream, which was made in the corridor immediately outside the *Pets' Corner*. The first time it was on sale after so long, we queued for a couple of hours, and the queue had to part now and then to let the pony rides through on their route. Paula and I bought two ice creams each, and licked them blissfully in turn. One small boy had his cone snaffled by a large dog, and wouldn't stop screaming.

Here, in Jaywick, there was a rather tacky general stores, where we bought an ice cream in the morning, and were treated by our dads to another in the afternoon.

I bought lots of saucy post-cards to send back to my pals: these often had the slogan: 'Meet you at your convenience.' We knew all about conveniences, for didn't our mums always find a spot on the sands immediately in front of the *Ladies*? This convenience appeared on most of our holiday snaps... Perhaps I should have collected these post-cards, rather than send them out, as they might be worth a bit after all these years! I also couldn't resist slotting a sixpence in the newly installed juke box – always the same tune: TEMPTATION or was it JEALOUSY? We listened to this as we danced our way down on to the sands.

We were always among the first on the beach. We'd had an early awakening be-cause, amazingly we could hear the rallying call from Butlin's Holiday Camp in Clacton – 'Wakey, Wakey Campers – Rise and Shine!' Jim groaned and said, 'Now you know why we won't take you *there* on holiday! Anyway, you couldn't have stood up to the Physical Jerks!' I had a cheeky reply: 'But *you* might have won the knobbly knees contest!' Jassy whispered to me, 'And you could've been Miss Bathing Beauty in your new costume!' Flattery that worked, as I treated her to a Sno-fruit, the forerunner of the ice lolly.

On our second day on the beach, we were making a sandcastle for Nick, while the two dads read their papers in deckchairs, with the legs of their trousers rolled up in case the tide came in unexpectedly, and in Jim's case, a clean white handkerchief knotted at the corners to protect his bald head from the brilliant sun, when we spotted the donkeys plodding along the sand nearby. The owner was touting for custom: 'You youngsters want a ride?'

Jassy and Nick were lifted up on to the

smaller donkeys, and I was allotted a larger animal. We had our ride, and as we returned saw a waiting crowd of children, mostly toddlers. The donkey man turned to Jassy and me. 'How'd you like to lead the donkeys with the little 'uns aboard?'

The dads agreed, while our mums probably would have not. For an hour at a time, with a rest between, we trudged tirelessly up and down. Our reward came at the end of the afternoon. 'Would you like to ride in the middle of the pack, home to Clacton?'

'Oh please,' we pleaded to Molly and Dolly, who had joined us with a packed lunch to be eaten in the open.

'Well...' Then Russ and Jim rose to the occasion. 'We'll walk the dog along the beach to meet you coming back, eh?'

'They'll be about an hour,' said the donkey man hopefully.

I was glad I was wearing shorts, like Jassy. Mine were borrowed from a Girl Guide friend, and were more a divided skirt, with box pleats. It was actually rather hair-raising, for the donkeys didn't plod as they did during the rides, but moved en masse very fast indeed, anxious to get back to the stables and their feed. That first time, we clung on, but as we were hemmed in by grey, hairy bodies, there was no chance of being thrown off our steeds.

At the end of the week we were unexpectedly paid a few shillings and then came the highlight of the holiday: we went to a Butlin's open evening with the rest of the family and the entrance fee entitled us to some free rides! We went on the Big Wheel, the Carousel, and the swing boats. *Steel Stella*, the roller coaster would have to wait for another year, our parents said.

The following year, we went there again, but I was too old to ride the donkeys by then. I spent most of my days glumly in the bungalow, writing cards to all my friends, saying I was having 'a wonderful time.' I don't think I even had a paddle in the sea. Typical teenager, I suppose.

Saturday evenings were spent, after the donkey summer, with Paula next door, while she listened out for her young brother, who was so good, we never heard a peep out of him, for our mothers were enjoying a night out in the church hall, at a whist drive! Paula's dad went too, but Jim wasn't one for cards, and he said Molly deserved a break. David was usually out and about too: the club was in the table tennis league.

Paula's dad was what Molly and Dolly called 'A fine figure of a man.' He had joined the newly formed Flying Corps in the First World War as a P.T. instructor. Paula told me that he'd been injured and had a steel plate in his crown. She didn't tell me exactly where this was located but it was an intriguing subject. The war wound meant that he was in a reserved occupation during the recent conflict. He was a very pleasant man, and he had an interesting job, in publicity for Odham's Press in London. Every weekend he brought home a pile of magazines and newspapers.

I'm afraid I wasn't very scintillating company for Paula. This reading matter was largely untouched by the young Motts, but I fell upon it with glee. We were supposed to be listening to the wireless, Max Jaffa and the Palm Court Orchestra, *In Town Tonight!* and *Saturday Night Theatre*, with Cecily Courtneidge and Jack Hulbert. I did listen to the play, but otherwise I was reading all the magazines. I flicked through *Picture Goer* with interest, My favourite was *John Bull*. The politics passed me by, but I found the serials absorbing. In the pages of *John Bull* I became acquainted with H.E. Bates – and have loved his writing ever since.

Paula sighed and looked fed up. She went out into the kitchen to make us supper. She wasn't allowed to cook, but she had her speciality: triple decker sandwiches, one layer marmite, the other sandwich spread.

Not surprisingly, she rebelled against staying in on Saturday evenings. Being a year ahead of me, she wanted to dress up, to go dancing, and to meet boys.

So, Paula went out with her friends and left me behind. That turned out to be the parting of ways for us, we had outgrown each other, I suppose.

'*You'll* have to learn to dance,' Molly said, when I moaned. David had been to the same ballroom dancing school as Paula, but I'd never had the inclination to join him. Molly decided, unbeknown to me, to call on Maggie's mum and to ask her if Maggie would be allowed to accompany me to Taylor's Academy. She said yes.

I never really mastered the tango, although Maggie and I practiced often, or reached the heights of my brother, who achieved gold medal standard, but Maggie and I blossomed to the strains of Victor Sylvester. 'Everyone gets a partner!' was little Miss T's rallying call. She was partnered by her niece, Joyce. They were super teachers and full of enthusiasm. God Bless them both!

The studio was the top floor of the house. There was a sprung dance floor, which had to be chalked before each lesson. We had to wear proper dancing shoes with leather soles. I was really upset when Jim, as he always did, applied a rubber sole (you could buy these at Woolworths) to my new special shoes. 'How can I wear them now?' I cried. He was upset too.

'Stop grumbling!' Molly said, but she bought me another pair.

There were separate cloakrooms for boys and girls. Ours was like a boudoir, with face-powder in cut glass bowls, clean powder puffs, to deal with shiny noses; long mirrors and flowers. Maggie and I always looked to see if anyone was wearing the same dress as us – it only happened once, thank goodness, to me. The girl concerned said cheerfully, 'Snap!' and I hid away in the alcove in the studio, instead of sitting on one of the chairs round the dance floor, waiting for a partner.

Miss T wasn't having any wallflowers. She despatched Big Tel to ask me to partner him in a waltz. He was a lofty chap, but very kind, and when we turned a corner, he lifted me effortlessly off my feet and twirled me round, which made me feel very special.

The boys, in turn, rushed to turn the handle of the gramophone, when the music began to slow down. We had all the latest tunes, but they were always recorded by Victor Sylvester, so you could mutter quick, quick, slow, one, two, three, etc. When it came to the last waltz, the lights were dimmed, and so no-one noticed that Maggie and I were dancing together... 'Hear the music of the waters,' we sang, 'softly come and softly go ... come back to Sorrento...'

We loved Taylor's academy, and we were soon attending local dances and feeling confident. We also met boys! They were all very well-mannered and in the interval, they treated us to tea and buns. No alcohol – and the evening always ended at eleven p.m.

That Christmas, the teachers planned a lovely surprise. The Upper School were joined by hand-picked (I suspect) boys from another local school for a joint Christmas dance. I had a pink crepe dress, and a trace of Tangee Natural lipstick. In the cloakroom, I removed the hated bows from my bunched hair, and combed it loose. All evening, girls complimented me on my 'lovely hair.' I refused to tie it back ever again, and like the rest of my class, I felt liberated and grown up.

Pride comes before a fall they say, as you will see...

TEN

Life Itself Is A Roller-Coaster

1947 was a year of ups and downs, not unlike *Steel Stella*. There was the exciting news of a Royal Wedding, but we had to wait until November for that. John and I still hadn't met yet, but he was off to do his National service that month in the R.A.F., and on 20th November, recalls being on a train to his first camp, looking out on flags flying in gardens. It was a foggy, sleety day in the north. He did get a slice of cake, on his arrival, but it wasn't wedding cake and like the other young men he was about to grow up quickly.

It began with the Christmas Holidays before and after the New Year. Our beloved grandfather had died in 1946, and how we missed his joyful exuberance. We didn't converge on the old Swan as usual, but stayed with Dolly and family in the cottage in Suffolk. Our grandmother was naturally sad, and despite all our efforts, we felt the same. It was the end of an era. Tilly, our youngest aunt, reunited with her husband after six years apart while he was in the Army, was overjoyed though, to be pregnant at last.

In freezing weather in February, there was a new little girl cousin to join Laura, me and Jassy. Dolly, who helped with the confinement at Tilly and her husband's home near Southwold, recalled 'nappies like stiff boards had to be wrenched from the line, and we were all, oh, so very cold...' I knitted baby Susie some pea-green booties, and Molly made a matinee outfit.

At school, there was some serious revision to be done, with Mock Matric examinations looming. It was 'heads down, no talking' time. Outings at this time for Maggie and me were a Saturday afternoon at the Pavilion, when we forgot our worries about the exams with viewing all the romantic pictures of the time; we were great fans of Joan Crawford, Bette Davis and Cary Grant – I also liked Van Johnson, and sent off for his picture and autograph. We weren't so keen on Abbott and Costello, or even Laurel and Hardy, but I've appreciated the latter for many years, since their films appeared on T.V. We enjoyed the musicals in colour, too. Who remembers Carmen Miranda with her sky-scraper hats piled with tropical fruit? The Pav was known as the Flea-Pit, so we were careful not to lean back in our seats. I can still conjure up instantly the mixed aromas from the Pav, some of them not too pleasant, despite the cheap disinfectant lavished in the Gents. Once, a woman in our row was joined by her husband, just back from work. She had his dinner, hot and steaming in a wrapped casserole dish on her lap. He spooned up stew and we were overwhelmed by the smell of onions. Oranges were another favourite, and the crunching of boiled sweets disturbed our concentration.

We still had our weekly dancing lessons, but Saturday night dancing was restricted for a while due to our studies.

One day we had pork for school lunch. Mine was pink and obviously tough and undercooked. I wasn't sick at the time, and I didn't hear that anyone else was affected by this dinner. Next morning, I woke feeling extremely ill. I staggered out of bed, and on passing the wardrobe mirror, noticed that my face had swelled, and that I had a rash too. I don't remember much of the ensuing days, except the doctor coming (a very rare occurrence) and that he thought it was either acute food poisoning, or perhaps glandular fever. I lay in bed, burning up, and the doctor's perplexity continued. I had some puzzling symptoms. Blood tests were not routine then.

I was actually away from school for a couple of months, but then it was the summer holiday, which thankfully meant no more time off, while I was slowly convalescing. In photographs of that time I am wearing a green and white cotton frock which Molly bought me from Marks and Sparks to cheer me up. It was from their first rail of clothes on sale after the war. I loved that dress because I was the first to wear it. It was very simple, with cap sleeves and horizontal stripes. We still had clothes coupons, but they would be one of the first things to go, and the *New Look* and longer hemlines was just around the corner...

In September, I returned to school, very lethargic and not really up to doing so. Then disaster struck. First, my skin began to peel all over, just as it had done after scarlet fever, but there was worse to come. My hair fell out in handfuls. The Head took me aside after Morning Assembly and then I learned how kind she could be, under her tough facade. I wept about my growing bald patches, and she comforted me. I was about to appear in a school production of *She Stoops to Conquer*, and the staff decided to hire me a wig to wear. It was just the boost I needed. I got a rousing reception for my part.

I no longer had long, blonde wavy hair – I had a thin, miserable straggle, which my school friends tactfully didn't mention. However, the hair loss ceased, and new hair began to grow in tight curls which was such a relief, apart from the fact that it was a different shade, more chestnut, like my brother's colour. Molly took me to the hairdresser. She helped me to come to terms with my changed appearance; my hair was cut very short and I looked very different with my bubble-cut.

Fortunately I couldn't know that the

mystery illness would have repercussions many years later. I went on to have a large family, as I'd hoped, and ignorance is indeed bliss!

Molly who had been shopping one afternoon, followed Maggie and me down the High street after school. She said later, that it had been a real tonic to her to hear us giggling all the way, as girls together tend to do. Dear Maggie kept my spirits up at that time, and when I went back to the dancing school, I never lacked a partner and nor did she – we were growing up fast.

David had been in the cadets at school, which was good experience for him, with his national service days coming up the following spring. He even had a girlfriend who took him out on the back of her motor-bike: he was saving up for a bike of his own. When he achieved his ambition, he monopolised the small kitchen with motorcycle parts on newspaper, and even, on occasion, the monster itself, propped against the table. We had a lot of arguments at that time: I couldn't bear the grease and the smell of some gunk he cleaned his hands with, or even the sight of him polishing his boots, or winding his puttees round his legs. He retaliated by telling Molly that I hadn't cleaned my shoes for weeks. (True.) I do regret having greeted one of his many mates at the door when I called out to my brother: 'One of your funny friends!' I met this particular chap much later and he confided: 'I was terrified of you!' What me? I was no doubt thinking, why do I always have to blush? JD didn't bear me a grudge, I'm told that he reads all my books!

I was eager to go up to London and to camp out on the pavement along the route of the Royal Wedding coach. Jim had a more practical idea. 'You'd have a better view of the passing parade from my office, and at least you'd be dry; rain is forecast for the 20th.' So Jim, Molly and I travelled up very early and I took a notebook to record my impressions. We were given seats by the window. It was an upstairs room, which was lucky as you could look down on the scene. As we ascended the grand staircase in the Admiralty, Jim observed: 'I can remember a young Jimmy Hogg sliding down the banisters here!'

The last time I had been in my dad's office, I was six years old, and the 'young ladies' kept me busy with paper and pencils, drawing them at work. I intended to do plenty of sketching this day, and writing, too.

The newspapers' special editions, published throughout the day, reported that Princess Elizabeth was also up early, looking out of her window in her dressing gown, and I imagined, perhaps with rollers in her hair, before the long preparations to transform her into a bride, began. She was just 21, and her prince five years older, so it seemed to us the stuff of fairy tales, a real romance. We toasted their happiness in Admiralty tea.

I was glad that I wasn't shivering on the wet, cold pavement and drinking lukewarm tea. The rain had thankfully ceased just after dawn, so the crowd in Whitehall were stretching cramped limbs, yawning, and then rolling up soggy blankets and bedding, to make room for more arrivals. Soon they were standing in a solid mass, excited and cracking jokes. Sober ministerial cars were cheered. We were eager for the music to begin: I could glimpse children, pushed to the front, so that they could see the processions, sitting on the kerb, munching breakfast rolls. An old lady, perhaps suffering from hypothermia, was lifted on to a stretcher and carried away by the first aiders. Bobbies moved the crowd back, with courtesy and encouraging banter.

First the Royal Marines, then the R.A.F. marched along, then grouped to play the National Anthem in honour of Princess Elizabeth's grandmother, Queen Mary, widow of King George V, who was in the first carriage, which was followed by Royal guests from other countries. In the office, we all scrambled to our feet, and stood to

147

attention, just as we did when the anthem was played in cinemas. The loudspeakers relayed the band music loud and clear.

The cheering from the crowd alerted the window watchers: the bridegroom in his car, smiling, and seemingly relaxed, resplendent in his naval dress uniform. The glass coach with Queen Elizabeth and the chief bridesmaid, Princess Margaret Rose followed, escorted by the Household Cavalry on their black horses. The bells pealed in the Abbey. The wedding ceremony was due to begin at eleven o'clock.

Windsor greys drew the state coaches and at last, the crowd had their reward, the first sight of the bride in her golden coach, but not her magnificent wedding dress, for this was covered by a fur coat, draped round her shoulders to keep her warm. Her father, the King, sat beside her and a voice behind me said softly, 'Oh, he looks so proud...'

The service was broadcast round the world, and we, too crowded round the wireless. We would later relive the occasion at the cinema, and the newspapers were no doubt kept as souvenirs – they certainly were in our house. We had a change in government, rationing was still in place, Britain was struggling back to normal, the big cities which had taken the brunt of the bombing, would never look the same, but the Royal Wedding made us optimistic for a better future.

We shivered constantly in the bitter winter which followed. Coal was like gold dust. John and I could well have met, but it was not time for that yet, when we both queued outside a local depot, when the rumour went round that they had a supply. We trudged through snow with our precious sacks in old prams or boxes on wheels.

Molly queued endlessly too – we had some bright pink sausages for supper one night, she didn't reveal that they came from the horse-meat shop. We may hear now that we had the perfect diet, but I would disagree: we were always hungry. Even bread, which had never been rationed in the war, was, for a while, available only with B.U.'s (bread units.)

I returned, initially reluctantly, to the fold – we had a new vicar at the parish church, and attendance was back to pre-war levels. My parents wanted me to be confirmed in the Anglican church The vicar had been brought up a Methodist, so the two churches often had joint services which Maggie began attending with me. Now we were considered young women, not children, we bought our first hats, *beanies*! We were inseparable at that time, and are still close, although we live too far apart, and both have family commitments, to meet up. She supported me enormously through that roller coaster year. Thank you, Maggie.

ELEVEN

Moments Of Glory

Collecting waste paper during and after the war years was something I tackled with enthusiasm. I met some interesting people when I knocked on their doors, something children were not usually encouraged to do, for obvious reasons. I suppose Molly didn't mind, because my 'regulars' were usually middle-aged women who enjoyed a chat with my friends and me, or elderly couples, shuffling to the door in slippers. They not only parted with ancient newspapers, they sometimes had a treat in store for com-pulsive readers, like bulky pre-war comics, which they presented with: 'You might like to read 'em, before they go in the sack...' I didn't feel guilty then, at smuggling these up to my bedroom.

'Who are you writing to?' Molly enquired one evening, as I dipped my pen in green ink – I tried all the colours before I settled on blue-black.

'A girl on this page-' I indicated a colourful comic, 'is asking for a pen friend...' I must have been about eleven, and loved writing letters.

'Look at the date on the front page,' Molly advised. 'She is probably about thirty years old by now!'

A school story is a school story, and it didn't occur to me that the illustrations were all of girls with shingled hair wearing gymslips with lots of pleats and belted low on the hips. The comic had been published before I was born!

I actually loved books from this era and earlier too. When Lily came to us, she brought a case with all her worldly goods. She'd been orphaned at an early age, and the only thing she seemed to have from her old home, was a couple of books. *Little*

Women and *Good Wives*. She lent me these books soon after she arrived. When she left us to marry Bob, she said: 'I would like you to keep my books, Sheila.' In turn, I passed them on to our elder daughter, Sara, who shared them with her sisters. It's only recently, that I realised how precious these dog-eared volumes must have been to Lily.

Maggie was with me at a later date, when we were invited into a large house and taken into a drawing room, dusty and rather oppressive, with heavy Victorian furniture and rather grim paintings on the walls. There was a stack of boxes on the window seat. 'I am packing up the ornaments – this place is too much for me to keep up, now – I can't afford to heat it properly, for one thing,' the old lady told us. She indicated what I thought was a piano. 'Have you heard one of these play?'

We shook our heads, not sure what she meant.

'Come closer, and watch what happens,' she invited us, lifting the lid.

She inserted a roll of what looked like parchment, pierced with holes. 'This, girls, is a pianola – listen – this is probably the last time I will play it...'

We saw the keys rise and fall, unstruck by human hand. The music was beautiful, as if played by a classical pianist. We were spell-bound.

A great sheaf of the musical sheets was thrust in our hands. 'Take it. It's just waste paper now.' The lid was closed on the pianola. 'It will probably make good fire-wood.'

A moment of glory, over.

This is more a gory moment: I was suddenly summoned to hospital to have my tonsils removed. I actually had to have the oper-ation twice, due to bleeding excessively on the first occasion, and didn't arrive home the next day as planned. Molly visited me to cheer me up – I was in the children's ward, but my feet stuck out of the end of the small bed – and she gave me a large bunch of grapes. In my dopey state, I ate all these after she left. Consternation from the nursing staff: 'Were there pips? You didn't have permission to eat anything yet!' I had to admit, I had no idea if they had pips or not, but I'd swallowed the lot.

I was brought home eventually by ambulance, which had to stop twice so that the nurse could deal with me being very sick. I had to be carried indoors on a stretcher. Molly put me straight to bed. However, after a week I was much better and able to return to school.

A few weeks later, came my second 'op.' This was just a matter of removing 'tags.' I was told: 'Your tonsils may grow again.'

'I'm not going back in hospital, even if they do!' I said firmly.

I was five feet two inches tall when I had the tonsillectomy, and suddenly I grew two more inches, much to the family's surprise. At last I was among the Big Girls in my class!

AEC had an announcement to make after registration one day. 'All schools in the area are invited to submit pupils' essays in a competition, sponsored by the local newspaper. There are several categories, according to age, and I hope that you will all write something. The best essays will be entered. The subject is "Waste Paper."'

There were a few groans: 'What can we write about *that*?' To me, those words were a spur. I would find out what happened to the waste paper after it was collected. I was already an avid researcher, and the encyclopaedias would help!

I wrote my essay in pencil, because I could keep up better with my thoughts, than dipping pen into ink – blots were always a drawback. Dialogue has always been part of my writing, and I didn't plan the essay, just let it flow. Maggie was part of the story, of course, and our forays in collecting the waste paper over the years. I found out about papier mâché, which resulted in more craft work for us, and how the paper was pulped and recycled. Once written, I stuffed the untidily written papers in a dressing table drawer.

The deadline drew nearer, and AEC requested that all essays be handed in. I forgot to bring mine and only remembered to hand it in on the last day. At lunch time, I was summoned to the Head's office. Miss C brandished my pencil scrawled papers: 'Disgraceful! You must write this out again in ink – now!'

It took me all lunchtime and an hour after school, to copy the essay on to fresh paper in my best handwriting. With a sigh of relief, I passed it to AEC, patiently standing by. 'Just in time,' she observed in relief. She had stayed to check my writing and would deliver our essays to the paper personally first thing next day.

Relieved, I promptly put this experience behind me, or so I thought.

We didn't have the local news delivered with the daily paper, Molly always bought it from the newsagents later in the day. That way, she got to read it before I crumpled it up! At least she didn't sit on it as Jim's father had done, to prevent the family opening the paper first!

I was mystified when I was greeted one morning at school by whispered 'Congratulations!' during registration. I was reprimanded for hissing: 'What for?' I didn't find out until later.

Then came my own moment of glory.

Into the classroom swept Miss C, carrying a folded newspaper in one hand, and we all stood to attention, chanting 'Good Morning!' I became aware that all eyes were on me again, that everyone was smiling, even Miss C. Then there was much clapping of hands, before the Head indicated that she wished to speak to us.

'I see you already know that congratulations are due to Sheila, who is the overall winner of the essay competition. There were over 3,000 entries. You look surprised, Sheila-'

'I am.' I said truthfully.

'You didn't see the paper earlier?' she queried.

'No...'

I expect you can guess who came second – the Head Girl! Miss C was pleased that several of 'our girls' had done well. We would be presented with our prizes at the Town Hall by the Mayor, we were told.

However, nothing could surpass this moment of glory for me, except maybe, the publication of my first book, *Tilly's Family*.

I have been zealous regarding waste paper ever since.

Revising for the coming important examinations was now a most serious business. We were allowed to pair up and to study quietly unsupervised in the library or in certain areas where we would not be interrupted. Maggie and I chose the Sick Room. We took turns to lounge on the bed to answer questions from the other, sitting on the chair. We concentrated on absorbing facts; there was no giggling or messing around. This dedication paid off when we took our French oral examination before the written papers. We had to describe a painting. I'm not sure if it was a happy coincidence, or whether it was suggested to us, but we had visited the National Gallery shortly before, and conversed in French all day. We did get the giggles then when we were approached by a couple of French tourists, who spoke so rapidly we couldn't understand what they were saying! I expect our version of their language was very laborious!

One day, a careers adviser came into our classroom. We were all asked in turn if we had any idea what we wanted to do when we left school. Some girls were staying on to take the Higher School Certificate and hoped to go on to college. (University wasn't mentioned.) They wished to become teachers. The most popular choice was a career in nursing. As a squeamish person, that was not for me, although, nursing turned out to be a large part of my maternal duties later, with all the childhood ailments still rife, like measles, mumps and chicken pox… Some girls had still to make up their minds, but I knew exactly what I wanted to do. When it came to my turn, I said simply: 'I want to be a writer.' The adviser regarded me thoughtfully for a moment. Then she said kindly, 'But Sheila, are you aware there is still a shortage of paper?' Those words have been on my conscience ever since.

As for becoming a cub reporter on a newspaper, I gathered you had to be able to ride a bike! I felt very deflated, as no helpful suggestions were made.

Later, I would find that the biggest drawback was not being able to type or take shorthand. Nowadays, with computers in schools, students learn how to use a keyboard when they are very young. Our school was academically excellent, but most of us continued our studies after we left, in order to secure employment, for jobs were like gold dust then. I went to evening classes for several years.

The examinations were not as fearsome as I expected. I remember the joy when I looked at the history paper and saw that I had revised all the right information! I did my best with the mathematics, but I knew I would never work in a bank. When it was all over, we awaited our results, and happily for me, like the rest of the class, I had done well, in particular in English Literature English Language, Art, History and French. I failed Domestic Science by a single point – I wasn't surprised at that, because when washing a cabbage under the tap, I inadvertently sprayed the Invigilator with cold water. My heart sank, when I saw her grim face and the way she stabbed her comments on my inefficiency with her pencil in the notebook. My brandy snaps unrolled in the cooking, too.

The only things I really remember about Domestic Science were, like the rest of the group, eating an illicit 'pinch' of 'raspings' from the big jar in the pantry (these were stale breadcrumbs baked in the oven, and tasted as if they were very ancient), and being caught standing in the bath in the flat to clean the taps. On that occasion, the teacher ignored the paddling, and ran her finger along the top of the bathroom door, then held the digit under my nose accusingly. 'You didn't clean up there!' Perhaps this is the moment to reveal that my family consider me a good cook! This is thanks to my mother, mother-in-law, husband – and grandmother's cook book. All our children are excellent at the culinary art, too.

We then looked forward to our final Prize giving. For the last time, our voices were raised in *Linden Lea*, and we had our moment of glory, when our results were announced. In turn, we went up to receive our certificates. Autograph books were signed, promises were made to keep in touch, to meet up. Our class photograph was taken. We all appear so fresh faced, and happy.

I didn't want to leave school, and asked Molly if I might stay on. 'It's not too late, other girls have changed their mind,' I pleaded.

'You say you don't want to go to college,' she reminded me.

'No, but...'

'It's time you grew up,' she told me, 'went out into the world. You can't be a schoolgirl for ever.'

It seemed to me she was unfeeling then, but she was right. David was already 'off hand' and Molly wanted more freedom too. She was only 40 years old.

It was my last day at school. Dear AEC told me: 'I shall have to buy a new bookcase to hold all your books.' I never saw her again, though we kept in touch, and she remembered me on my wedding day. FF said, 'I knew you could do it!' I was fortunate to meet up with her from time to time, and have a bundle of her letters.

I had already attended one job interview, at the BBC, with Maggie. Several other girls from our class were selected to apply. This was quite exciting, but there were only clerical positions available. However, we soon discovered that the first two girls interviewed secured the jobs. Mr Mott kindly offered to see if there were any openings in the publishing business. However, Molly took this the wrong way and told me, 'We don't want to be beholden to them'. I think the real drawback was that Mrs Mott was sometimes patronising to my mum. I don't think she meant to be, in fact they worked tirelessly together as volunteer helpers for the local Darby and Joan Club, even when they were older than many of the members!

Maggie and I were now seriously seeking employment. We were both sad we would no longer see each other every day, but we would meet up to go to the Pictures one evening in the week, there were the Saturday night dances – we might even go to the new dance hall, we decided. We would continue with our Saturday shopping in Croydon or Streatham, and church on Sunday mornings.

During that final school summer holiday,

we walked often down the Green Lane to the Grove, where we practised our serves with two elderly tennis racquets and a tired, rather bald ball. We were great Wimbledon fans. There was also a day trip to Brighton, when I was invited to go there with Maggie and her family. It was a lovely day, we travelled by train, and ate our picnic lunch on the pebbled beach, enjoying the spray as the sea rushed in and foam tickled our bare feet. We girls were keen to have a paddle (neither of us could swim.) We were waist deep and crying, 'Ooh!' as the cold water lapped round us, when Maggie suddenly disappeared – the beach shelved sharply at that point. She came up spluttering, but thankfully laughing, and we beat a hasty retreat to the shore. We were walking back along the beach as it would soon be time to catch the excursion train home, when we heard a voice booming through a megaphone. 'Last trip of the day!' We went out in a motor boat as the sun set and the colours were reflected in the water. A magic moment.

There was a former teacher who lived locally who was on the lookout for recruits to join the company in London where she was personnel officer. She had left teaching before I started school, but I knew her by sight, as she rode her bicycle to the shops. When I was trusted to go to the corner shop as a child, I was also trusted to 'look right, look left, look right again' by Molly. This I did in a most perfunctory manner, I'm afraid. Once I stepped out to cross the road, and this same lady almost ran over my foot and could have fallen off her bike. She seized my arm in a vice like grip and told me off in teacher-tones. I didn't tell Molly about this incident, but she did, so I was told off again. For some time I had a recurring nightmare about – what shall I call her? Miss P, will do… In my dreams she more resembled the Wicked Witch from The Wizard of Oz.

I digress: Miss P had obviously forgotten that I was once hopeless at road-drill. She was impressed by my examination results, and arranged an interview. She didn't discuss this with me, but with Molly.

'*Insurance!*' I cried, when I heard. 'I don't want to go – didn't Dad say I wasn't cut out for the Civil Service?'

'It's not the Civil Service–'

'I don't care! It sounds like figure work, anyway, and you know–'

'And I know, you have to start your working life somewhere!'

So I sat another examination, presided over by Miss P, and despite my misgivings I was offered a clerical position. Molly was pleased because it was a North American company and three course lunches were provided free of charge. There was also the lure of a food parcel at Christmas.

You will find out how I got on in the next chapter! Maggie, meanwhile, went to work in a local bank. We were lucky to find jobs at all, we were told.

TWELVE

Down Among The Dead Men

Molly insisted that we have the usual family holiday before I commenced commuting to London each day. The Insurance company wanted me to start work at the beginning of September, but that was the only time we could book the bungalow on the cliff at California, Norfolk. It was agreed I could join the company in the middle of the month. In retrospect, this was unfortunate, for several other girls had already been through the Initial training, before I arrived, and I would have to 'catch up.'

California has always been one of my favourite places. It has featured in two of my books, and in a short story, *'Californy Here We Come'*, published in *Woman's Realm*.

This was the song we sang as we motored there, having met up in Suffolk, to travel the rest of the way in our uncle's car.

In this further excerpt from *The Family at Number Five*, I describe a visit to California just before the outbreak of WW2.

The little car was bursting at the seams with all the baby paraphernalia. 'We'll have to make do with one pair of shorts and a couple of tops each, and hope to goodness it doesn't rain,' as Mirry told Fred and Glory. They were off on a summer holiday, the third week in August.

The chalet bungalow was almost teetering on the cliff edge, which caused Mirry to twitter anxiously, until Fred pointed out there would be four of them to keep an eye on Glory, when Bar and Clive arrived later in the day. They were travelling here on the motorbike. Anyway, Glory could be a sensible child when she chose, and there were steps carved out to the sandy beach below and a handrail which was, well, adequate. As for baby Beaulah, at six weeks old the only demands she would make were the middle-of-

*the-night 'Hurry up and feed me, Mum!' cries
and a long line of nappies blowing like white
flags against a perfect blue sky, for the swooping
seagulls to target and splatter.*

*They were on the east coast, in a windswept
place with far-reaching views, and the red flag
flying more often than not. But it was just the
place for shrimping, with plenty of rock pools for
Glory to paddle safely in, with water warmed by
the sun. In the lanes around, the scarlet poppies
waved among the long grass at the edge of the
fields, the sails of the tall white windmill turned
and the church spire gleamed gold like the corn.
Clusters of cottages with neat gardens with pea
sticks and sweet peas intermingled with cabbages
and cabbage roses. Wooden shacks, which were
dark and cool within, with fish laid out on
marble slabs, still bright-eyed and shiny. The post
office sold stamps and sweets and opened and
closed at the owner's whim. They were in Poppy
Land, Mirry fancied. She didn't know that was
what the locals already called the place...*

Young Cora, just released from hospital

after being very ill with diphtheria, in *The Gingerbread Girl*, is taken by her mother, Biddy's friend Eliza to California to convalesce. They travel by train... This part of the story is also set just pre-war. The novel was published by Hale, then in large print by Magna, and also in audio (Magna Sound.)...

Steam billowed, doors opened, folk disembarked. Porters appeared with trolleys to transport luggage. Cora and Eliza stood back until the chaos cleared, then Eliza helped her young friend aboard...

'Where are we going?' Cora ventured.

'Californy, here we come!' *Eliza sang out sweetly with a smile.*

'California, d'you mean? That's in* America!' *Biddy had a sister there...*

'This one's in Norfolk. Not far from Great Yarmouth, where I sent them bloaters from, last year...'

The final stage of their journey was in the early

evening. They bowled along the winding lanes by pony and trap, driven by Ginny Brookes, small and round like her sister, with a man's flat cap on a bundle of hair which was faded but still streaked with red.

'Look!' Eliza pointed out to Cora 'Californian poppies!' It was June, a bright, golden evening, and they caught glimpses of the sea below the cliffs before they veered inland.

'They're yellow,' Cora observed, 'not like the ones on 'memberance Day...'

California, the village, was much like that still in 1948. There was one important change, however: the erosion of the cliffs. There were DANGER! signs – including by our steps down to the beach, which were crumbling. We descended carefully, and when on the soft, fine sand it all seemed as before. It was to be our last family holiday there, unfortunately. Poppies, both red and yellow, still captivate the tourists. However, the bungalow we stayed in then, where Tikki the tabby pounced on lizards which wriggled away, leaving their tails behind, long ago toppled into the sea.

Jim took me as far as the impressive doors of the Insurance Company on my first morning. The bus stop was conveniently near the building. He kissed me 'good luck' and I waved him goodbye.

I could hardly complain of being on my own, for I was given a desk in a large room, open plan except for a glassed-in office at one end. The girls who were already established in the routine, eyed me superciliously. I recognised one from school, but she had been part of a different group of friends. She looked very grownup in a smart new outfit with plenty of makeup on her face. She wore sheer stockings and court shoes. I had a new coat, serviceable tweed, worn over a skirt and blouse; rayon stockings, which I kept up with elastic 'garters', disdaining a suspender belt, and school shoes. Molly had dabbed powder on my nose.

The supervisor obviously regarded me as a nuisance, for she had to repeat all her instructions to me, having finished training the first girls. They were already a team, and not keen to show me the ropes. I was given all the filing to do, while they went on to better things. I kept my head down to disguise the tears in my eyes and shuffled the great mound of papers. I had the feeling the supervisor wanted to punish me for taking a holiday before I even started work...

I didn't realise how fortunate I was to start work in surroundings which were much better than I might have experienced in other offices in post-war London. Desks, chairs and filing cabinets all appeared new. The latter were ranged along one wall, and during my first week when I pulled out one of the long drawers to file away the endless papers, the drawer slammed shut on my right hand. The pain was excruciating, but I didn't cry out, and not a head was raised to see my predicament.

I managed to free my hand, but the nail on

my forefinger was badly crushed. I felt as if I was going to pass out. I steadied myself and asked the supervisor if I might be excused. In the cloakroom I ran cold water over my bruised hand and then tied a clean hanky over the finger. I went back to my desk and wondered how I would get through the rest of the day. The supervisor, noting the improvised bandage, obviously guessed what had happened and commented: 'You must be more careful.' Vera, a middle-aged clerk who sat at the next desk, fetched me a glass of water and an aspirin. The damaged nail turned black and eventually came off; it was ages before I grew a new nail.

Vera was rather eccentric but after that kept a motherly eye on me. I valued her quiet advice. 'We all started with filing, dear. Things will get better.' She invited me to join the 'sugar club.' We were provided with cups of tea mid morning, and again during the afternoon. These were delivered on a trolley by the tea lady, who allowed us two sugar lumps each. I took sugar in my tea then, so this was bliss. Vera opened a drawer and showed me a box almost full of sugar lumps. 'We save them until we have a couple of pounds then I take them to a shop where you can exchange the sugar for chocolates! We all put something in the kitty, because you have to pay for them, of course, new girls like you usually contribute sixpence a week. Would you like to join?' I couldn't say 'no', could I? Though I only received two chocolates from the first box, because there were so many members of the sugar club, it was worth all those cups of sugarless tea.

I knew that the glass box office was occupied by the Manager, but I never actually saw him arrive or leave. Various privileged members of staff, male, mostly, entered his sanctum occasionally. They were usually from Accounts, upstairs.

I met the Manager after I had another mishap. I broke my glasses. As I was fairly helpless without them, I was summoned to his office. He was of short stature, and not intimidating at all, a kindly man. He said: 'I have arranged for my optician to see you today, to supply you with new frames as your lenses are intact. Here is his card. You may leave work after lunch as you will have to travel to the West End, and then you are free to go home afterwards. How are you getting on with your work? I understand you are an artistic young lady.'

Who on earth had told him that? It surely wasn't relevant to insurance, I thought. Naturally, I fibbed, 'Very well thank you.'

He regarded me thoughtfully. 'We are short of staff in Accounts –would you be interested in moving up there temporarily? It is good to have a fresh challenge, a change of scene now and then...'

Even though I knew Accounts equalled mathematics, I had a lunch time friend Audrey, who worked upstairs, so I was indeed interested.

I still shudder at the thought of my journey into the unknown, i.e. the West End of London. It took me ages to find the superior opticians, not surprising if you can't see the number on the bus or decipher the destination. It was a consulting room, not fronted by a window full of spectacle frames as I expected.

Another little man with a nice smile, wearing a bow tie, treated me like royalty. I didn't like to tell him I wasn't too keen on horn-rimmed specs, because he said, with satisfaction: 'Ah, this is the pair for you. Very intellectual.' I just wanted to look attractive, that's all. I decided immediately I wouldn't wear the specs to dances.

It was late afternoon when I emerged from the shop, it would soon be dusk and I panicked. Even with the glasses, I had no idea where I could find the right bus stop home. I walked in one direction, then another: It was November, and there was the acrid smell of fog in the air. I found a phone and two pennies and rang the office. Would anyone still be there? The supervisor answered. 'Stay where you are,' she commanded 'and we'll come and get you.' She arrived after half-an-hour with Kay, the girl

I'd known at school, in tow. 'Kay will escort you home by train,' she said.

We had to stand in the corridor and weren't able to converse, but I was too embarrassed to talk anyway. We parted at the Clock Tower. I thanked her for her company and hurried home.

'Oh dear,' Molly exclaimed, 'I expect you'll get a big bill for those frames – why on earth didn't you ask to go home then we could have gone to our usual opticians?'

The bill eventually arrived, written by hand on thick, watermarked paper. £2-10 shillings. More than half one week's wages! I had to buy a postal order in order to pay it.

We were paid monthly, which meant I had to budget carefully for fares and housekeeping, but I was proud to be able to buy my mother a big bunch of mimosa to mark my launching into the business world.

Thankfully, I actually enjoyed my time in Accounts. I met other jolly girls about my age, but Aud, as we called her, was the general favourite. She was a thin girl, with black hair, green eyes and a very pale, freckled skin. She came from Golders Green. I was invited to her next birthday party there. We rolled back the carpet in the living room and placed her one and only record on the gramophone turntable. *'Put another record On, On the Nickelodeon,'* we sang along with Theresa Brewer. Aud was a live wire, full of fun. She showed us how to jive to the beat of the music.

However, she suffered from terrible boils, and sometimes I stood by her in the cloakroom at work as she sobbed with the pain of these monsters, one inside a nostril, as I recall, and another under her arm. She would dry her eyes, and smile, squeeze my hand, and say, 'Don't tell anyone, will you?' Her mother took her to the doctors but they couldn't offer much relief. Penicillin must have been available then, but it was the early days of the National Health Service. We lost touch when I moved on, but I do hope she had better health in later life. Where are you now, little Audrey Maynard?

Fortunately we had calculators in Accounts, but mostly what we did, was to stick stamps on receipts for instalments on policies received. Accounts wasn't dry and stuffy, it was a busy hive of chatter and laughter.

Another summons by the Manager. I had done well, he said, but would I be able to help out in the Vaults? This was known as Down Among The Dead Men.

I was to assist Anna, who was half-French, and, I was delighted to discover, a story-weaver like myself. It was rather alarming, on my first morning, to be escorted down steep stairs, with doors unlocked en route, to what seemed like a dungeon. When the last doors clanged shut behind us, we were in another world. The many boxes and files in here were not exactly covered in cob-webs, but were battered and often bursting at the seams. They were the dead claims, and some were labelled with famous names.

Anna had a long list of instructions. Sometimes she climbed a library ladder and handed down untidy parcels to me.

'These are deeds, wanted by a solicitor, when a will is read, or if there is a dispute over inheritance,' she informed me.

I was intrigued by crackling, yellowing pages and red wax seals. We placed our finds in boxes which would be collected at the end of the morning. We were escorted up the stairs at lunch time and back again after an hour.

'It's secret, I'm not allowed to talk about it,' I informed my friends as I sat blinking in the daylight. 'You're all dusty.' Aud brushed my hair with her hand.

My parents were not too happy about me working Down Among The Dead Men. 'It sounds unhealthy down there to me,' Molly worried.

The novelty was beginning to wear off, when Anna told me she was leaving at the end of the month. She was going to train as a house-mother in a children's home.

When I first started work, Jim suggested that I buy an evening paper after work: 'Something to read on the bus,' he said. He brought home the *Evening Standard*, and when David was at home, before he went off to the R.A.F., he chose *The Star*. The familiar cry of the corner newsvendors was: 'Star, News and Stannard!' So I was left with the *Evening News*, which was rather difficult to handle when opened out on the confines of the bus.

The *Standard* had classified ads, like job vacancies: I preferred my paper because of the daily story. Now, Jim drew my attention to an advertisement. 'Trainee Proof Reader wanted for Publisher.'

I'd achieved my first year with the Insurance Company, as I'd promised, Molly had been delighted with the Christmas parcel. I was fit and well due to all the nourishing meals. Time for a change. It sounded good to me.

THIRTEEN

Twelfth Street Rag

Meanwhile, Maggie was settling in at the bank. Despite her misgivings, she found the staff friendly, although they were older than her. A couple of the men had returned there after the war, as their positions had been kept open. The main drawback, she confided to me, was having to balance the books at the end of each working day. 'You're not allowed to go home until you've accounted for the very last halfpenny,' she sighed. Then she brightened up: 'If I don't get married for about ten years, I'll get a bonus when I do.'

'How can they expect you to wait *that* long?' I marvelled.

Maggie had to work Saturday mornings, I

was luckier in that respect in my first job. However the publishers worked longer hours, including some Saturdays, and there were no free meals, or cups of tea and sugar lumps...

We fitted in our shopping sprees when we could. Clothes were now coupon free, the New Look was here, and C & A had arrived in Croydon with up to the minute fashions! The pretty dresses were affordable, cotton and easy to launder; the skirts were full enough for twirling when dancing, we wore lace-trimmed petticoats from Dorothy Perkins and graduated to roll-on girdles. We cinched our small waists with wide belts with fancy buckles, which was a hazard if you were dancing with someone in uniform and your belts became 'attached.' We bought sandals from Bata (which didn't last long if you went out in wet weather) and in the winter, crepe soled fur-lined boots from Stead and Simpson. I later had a nasty accident in icy weather due to squidgy crepe soles. But that's a later story... Colour, it seemed to us, was coming back into our world.

Best of all, we had Saturday evenings at the Grandison Ballroom, just a tram ride away, with live music, including regular visits from Kenny Ball and his Jazzmen.

It took me some time after Saturday high tea, to prepare for the evening out. First, a bath, though I could never have a good soak as five inches of water was the rule – was that a government decree, or family economy? Then, draped in a towel, it was time for the Drene shampoo. This liquid in the bottle, which smelled similar to washing up liquid of today, had replaced the old Amami sachets of gritty, grey powder, and resulted in a lovely shine on your hair. The way we dried our hair was certainly rather danger-ous. Molly lit the gas oven on low, and I poked my head inside and 'flapped' my hair until damp-dry. She then encouraged the wave in my hair with her fingertips. It was a relaxing experience and the results were pleasing.

Make-up was applied before slipping my dress carefully over my head. I used Ponds cream as a foundation, face powder on nose and chin, Vaseline on eyelids and lashes, to make them glisten, and finally, lipstick. Maggie and I had graduated from *Tangee Natural*, an orange stick which changed colour on your lips and was indelible, to brighter shades: we both used the new lip 'pencils' and blotted our lips carefully with good old Bronco toilet tissue. Neither of us used mascara or eye shadow, after a disastrous evening when it rained and we had 'panda eyes' when the black ran. The final touch was perfume: my favourite was Muguet des Bois (Lily of the Valley to you!) I would tuck my glasses in my handbag after I left the house.

We sat side by side at the back of the hall, but we weren't wistful wallflowers, we chatted to each other in an animated fashion, and partners would appear. It seemed to us that they arrived in pairs, a tall chap and a shorter one. Very often, little Maggie was invited to dance by the taller boy, and I would be asked by the short one. I expect they wondered what on earth we were giggling about. Then, one evening Maggie met her match in Leslie, and it's strange but true, that she did indeed wait ten years – and gained the Bank dowry! – before she married him. He was older than us, and generously included me at refreshment time. He even took me along with them to the pictures on occasion! The small box of chocs was passed to me, too, and I overheard him whisper to Maggie: 'She's had the caramel!' I had my share of 'dates' too, but nothing serious. I didn't have the time, because I was attending night school twice a week, and still studying as well as working. When I met a date one evening at the cinema, he complained that I slept through most of the film! I'm afraid I did the same thing in the gallery at the Last Night of the Proms in the Albert Hall... My escort thought that was beyond the pale. I *almost* went out with a Wimbledon prospect –

David, who was a keen tennis player, was envious of my good luck. But 'almost' doesn't mean I took up the offer of playing mixed singles at a prestigious local tennis club – after all, Maggie and I had only practised serving, not perfected any other strokes. I had the white shorts, but I knew that was not enough... I made some feeble excuse and this handsome individual immediately lost interest in me. David said, 'I would have gone! Why didn't you tell him I'd like to play him?'

'Because you're not a girl,' I told him. He had no answer to that.

Dancing was a different matter – I loved it. The jive was becoming popular, but was frowned upon at that time. Eventually, the couples who couldn't resist this kind of dancing were permitted to perform their sometimes amazing contortions on one side of the dance floor. We often paused to watch, when in the middle of a waltz or foxtrot.

There was always a feeling of excitement,

of anticipation near the end of the evening when the Jazzmen were playing. A roll of drums, and the call: 'On your feet – Twelfth Street Rag, everyone!'

We surged on the floor, with or without partners, the music swept us up, we improvised the steps and sang along – it was a wonderful climax to our dancing.

If there was an encore, we sometimes missed the last tram home, but we trudged home under a starry sky and even if it was cold, or drizzly, we didn't care.

My new job was not far from Fleet Street, which I liked to walk along and dream of working in the hub of the writing world. However, this was a dingy office in a building which had suffered war damage, and faced demolition in the future. It was a large room, with rows of tables and un-friendly faces. The copy typists, all old hands, didn't welcome newcomers, particu-larly trainee proof readers, I gathered, because they were disgruntled that one of their number had not been offered this position. I certainly wasn't aware, until I was told much later, that I was paid more than them, from the start, which was unfair after all their years of service. I was assigned to a grim senior proof reader who wore an overall to keep her office clothes clean. She told me right away that she hadn't asked for an assistant but she supposed she'd have to put up with me, and I'd better learn quickly. She handed me a huge catalogue and told me to cut out every single advertisement and paste on to separate sheets of paper. 'These are often changed, and you will then make the relevant corrections,' she told me. The first thing I learned was 'stet' meaning same, or no change.

After a week of cutting-out, I had red ridges on my thumb and forefinger, but I battled on. Corrections were marked with a mapping pen. This was a business dictionary – the interesting part was designing new advertisements to the customer's directions. But, it wasn't the sort of publishing I had hoped for – magazines or books. Nevertheless I was learning the jargon, proofs and galleys, the symbols. My typing expertise came in handy, but I hadn't found a use for shorthand yet.

We ate our sandwiches in the rest room – which had a sagging sofa, a few hard chairs, no kettle, but a Burco boiler to heat the water for tea. We were provided with a pint of milk, and a quarter of tea, and that was it. The typists ignored me, and so did the more elevated staff, who all seemed to be related to the two men in charge, who had a cubbyhole office off the main room. I was not accepted as part of either group. The lavatories were awful. There was one on the end of the block, which was kept locked. Only the more privileged members of the staff had the use of the key. I got a glimpse in there, one day. This cubicle had a flowered pedestal and tiles on the wall – and toilet paper! We had to wash at the restroom sink and queue to look in the cracked mirror on the wall.

I did finally find a friend there. A young girl called Joy. We shared chocolate biscuits, with a delicious jammy centre from her father's grocery shop. We began going out at lunch-time, buying a milk shake at a milk bar, and eating our sandwiches, on a seat with pigeons hovering around. Joy didn't like it there any more than I did. We decided to try the Stella Fisher Employment Bureau. We both had interviews lined up. The one I went to, was on a newspaper. The man who saw me might have had the green shade over his eyes, but he also had his feet up on his desk, and he had big holes with his toes poking out of his socks. He also badly needed a shave, and he smoked cigars. 'Can you handle a switchboard?' he asked. When I said, 'No,' he lost interest and I beat my retreat. Joy was luckier, she was offered a position as a trainee photographer.

I began studying the Sits Vacant in Jim's paper. I spotted one for a comptometer on a women's magazine. I had no idea what a comptometer was, but I had visions of writing articles and short stories – when I was established, of course! For the first and last time in my working life I took an illicit sick day off. I caught the bus in good time for the interview, but things went wrong thereafter. The bus was stopped half-way, because a man refused, or couldn't pay his fare. The argument with the conductor seemed to go on for ages. In desperation, I tapped the shabby man on his shoulder and offered to pay his fare. The conductor advised against it, but I handed over four-pence, and to my relief the bus moved on. It had been a sunny start to the day, but when I alighted at my stop, there was a cloudburst and torrential rain. I was soaked to the skin, hair in rat-tails, shoes squeaking, and I was running late for my appointment. Needless, to say, I wasn't offered the job, I must have looked like a drowned rat, and by then the sun was shining again... I was also told there were no prospect of anything other than operating the machine, and they needed someone with experience. I didn't want to make another mistake, I decided. I knew it would upset my parents if I did. I kept quiet about how unhappy I was with such unsociable fellow workers, after Joy had left. We still met up at lunch times and that made it bearable. Then something happened which made life good again – *I met John*!

Maggie and Les had tickets for the United Dairies annual dance, to be held at Streatham Baths (The pool was covered in the winter, for such a purpose, and it was November, 1950.) They invited me to join them. I was to make my own way there, as Maggie was never sure what time she could leave the bank.

It was raining, and I wore my new mack, red, with white spots, with dinky white rubber boots. I had a red umbrella to protect my head and newly set hair. I shivered, because the mack wasn't as warm as an overcoat, and I was wearing a pretty, sleeveless blue crepe dress with cross-over bodice, fastened discreetly with a favourite Woolworth brooch, a little mermaid. People arrived, but hurried inside and there was no sign of my friends. I didn't want to go in on my own, and was considering catching the next bus home, when I was joined by a tall young man in a stylish white mack with the collar turned up. After a few minutes, I ventured to ask: 'Do you have the time on you?' Then I had the embarrassing thought that he might think I was 'picking him up' – something no well-brought up girl would do. However, he looked at his watch and replied politely, 'Almost eight o'clock. Are you waiting for someone?'

'My friends,' I said. 'They're late.'

'I'm waiting for friends too.'

Then both sets of friends arrived together, so we smiled at each other, and went inside.

'He looked nice,' Maggie said, excited for me. I'd been down in the dumps lately over my job. 'I bet he'll come over and ask you to dance!'

But he didn't – not until the interval waltz

that is. Not that I lacked partners. I danced with a Scotsman, an Irishman, and a Welshman in turn – so it was time for an Englishman to ask: 'Would you like to dance?'

We sat up on the balcony and talked over our tea and biscuits. We danced every dance together after that. However, we parted at the cloakrooms at the end of the evening, to collect our coats.

'Didn't he ask to see you again?' Maggie asked.

I shook my head, disappointed. But when we emerged to leave, he was waiting to ask me: 'Can I see you home?'

Maggie gave me a nudge, whispered. 'Go on – he's genuine, I can tell. And we'll be on the bus, too...'

John escorted me to my front gate. 'Can I see you again? Would you like to come to the pictures?' I said that I would. Then I told him to hurry or he'd miss the last bus back to Streatham.

I looked in on Molly and Jim, reading in bed. 'Did you have a good time?' she asked.

'Oh, I did! I met such a nice boy–'

'That's funny,' she said, 'I was just looking at wedding pictures in my magazine....'

'Oh, *Mum*!' I said.

FOURTEEN

Black-Eyed Susie

My fur-lined boots were great for keeping my feet warm when trekking through snow to work, after leaving the morning bus. The crepe soles were however, an accident waiting to happen... In the freezing conditions of January, soon after I met John, I came a cropper. One moment I was treading cautiously along, the next I was sliding helplessly at speed and smacked into an imposing edifice – the solid front wall of a bank, no less.

I came to, lying in a heap with a concerned

crowd round me. I looked up, trying to focus, and saw a coloured man, bending over me to check my injuries.

In my confused state, I thought: I've died and gone to Heaven...

The doors to the bank were opened and I was carried inside. There were more puzzling images. The bank staff attempting to help me, were all small people, and speaking in a language I couldn't understand. Much later I would learn that this was the Malaysian bank, that they had opened up before the usual time, and were doing their best to help. I was laid gently on a padded bench and questioned in English: 'What is your name, please? Who shall we contact? Do you need a doctor?' I opened my mouth, but couldn't answer.

A doctor was called, and said I was concussed. I came to sufficiently to tell them my father worked at the Admiralty, but I couldn't remember his number. 'You must not worry,' they said, 'We will contact him.'

Eventually, Jim arrived. He had caught a

later bus than me, but fortunately was in his office when the telephone rang. He decided to take me home, because by then I was sitting up, though very groggy and he could see that I was going to have a black eye. The bank staff made us hot, sweet tea to fortify us for the journey.

There were no taxis to be hailed, it had to be the bus. I leaned against my dad and closed my eyes. 'What's wrong with your right arm?' he asked me, alarmed. It hung limply at my side, but didn't hurt then. 'Bruised,' I murmured.

Molly put me to bed, and my arm in a sling. I could move my fingers, so they thought it wasn't broken. The doctor said he would come first thing in the morning if needed. He was rushed off his feet with minor accidents that day. 'A couple of aspirin and a hot water bottle' was his advice.

The doctor sent me to the hospital the following morning for X-rays. Molly and I spent most of the day there. I had broken my collar bone and dislocated my shoulder. Eventually I returned home with the injured arm immobilised across my chest with a giant strip of elastoplast. Only my hand was free, but unusable from that position. I would have to struggle left-handed. Ruefully, I thought of the ambidextrous twins at school. Because of the concussion, I was told I must rest for several weeks and would be signed unfit for work.

The firm was unsympathetic. After a couple of weeks I was asked to show myself in the office so that they could see I was really incapacitated! They were also reluctant to pay me the sick benefit to which I was entitled.

This clinched matters for me. I would return to work, in due course, but I would definitely leave there as soon as I could.

John was a great support, and when Maggie's little mum asked me: 'Is he the One?' I beamed, and said simply, 'Yes!'

From then on, once I was working again, John left his home, some miles away, very early, turned up at our house just after breakfast, and escorted me to the door of that dismal building. He did this in reverse in the evening. It was wonderful to be young and in love. We've been together ever since.

I met his family – and we all got on splendidly. Still do. John and I have a lot in common, our ever-increasing family of course, and art, books, love of country living. We have had an adventurous life together. We differ in some things – he is keen on most sport, and when he was younger participated in it, too. He is more practical than me, but we mix and match, as it were...

Stella Fisher came up trumps. She passed me a card. 'These are well respected publishers, lovely people, they intend to move to premises in Holborn soon, so don't be put off by the present building.'

She was right. Butterworths were a super firm to work for. It wasn't quite what I hoped for, as they published medical and law books, but it was civilisation.

Hooray! I joined an office of five other girls, as a junior secretary.

Breams Buildings – is it still in existence? – was in Fetter Lane, and the exterior was unpromising. There was an old-fashioned lift (which 'appears' now and again in my stories, plus the liftman, Fred Head – both affectionately recalled, I have to say) He had a powerful pull on the rope which swung the cage upwards, despite having lost an arm in the war. He was the most cheerful chap, and what we now refer to as a 'people person.' There was a notice in Fred's lift, which intrigued me the first time I read it. SHOULD YOU LOSE YOUR RIGHT GLOVE, I SHOULD BE GRATEFUL FOR THE OTHER. He wore out a lot of gloves on that rope.

The large room where I joined my new colleagues was freshly painted and the desks were all by the windows, except for the office boy, who sat with his back to the girls and ear-wigged on our conversations. He was a nice lad, and told me cheerfully one day, 'When I'm manager, you shall be my secretary!'

Part of my duties were to act as assistant to the manager's secretary, Nita, a beautiful girl of Italian origin. She was a great fan of Arsenal football club, living in Little Italy. I took dictation mostly from the Major, who, like the Manager, had his own office adjacent to ours.

There was Lilian, who was married to a regular in the airforce, Valerie, Ann and Joan, who worked with Phyllis (who also had her own small office) and at break times we linked up with more friends from the other side of the corridor. There was another office where the editors and copywriters worked and later I would join them. Most of these were older than us, but lively and interesting women.

The first day when everyone disappeared for lunch, I suddenly wondered what I should do. We were given luncheon vouchers, only 1/6d. but welcome all the same. Then Joan, who had been busy all morning, but smiled at me now and then from her desk opposite, spoke. 'Would you like to come out to lunch with me?'

So I found a kindred spirit – a girl like me, always reading, who apologised for propping her current book against the salt pot on the ABC cafe table, but who walked with me after our tomato soup, bread roll, plain yoghurt and cup of tea (which used up all the voucher!) and took me down all the little streets full of history which she had already discovered. We are friends to this day.

Terry, the office boy, tailed John and me in the mornings, when he walked me up the office as usual, until we moved to Holborn, and said later: 'Cor, he looks like Dick Barton, Special Agent in that white mack!'

This is a short chapter, but a happy ending. I became engaged while I was at Butterworths, and well, those of you of who have read *Knee Deep in Plums*, will know what happened next...

The publishers hope that this book has given you enjoyable reading. Large Print Books are especially designed to be as easy to see and hold as possible. If you wish a complete list of our books please ask at your local library or write directly to:

Dales Large Print Books
Magna House, Long Preston,
Skipton, North Yorkshire.
BD23 4ND